True Living Organics

2nd Edition

The Ultimate Guide to Growing All-Natural Marijuana Indoors

The Rev

Green Candy Press

True Living Organics: The Ultimate Guide to Growing
All-Natural Marijuana Indoors, 2nd Edition
Published by Green Candy Press
Toronto, Canada

www.greencandypress.com

ISBN: 9781937866099

Cover photo: © DoobieDuck, www.doobieduck.com and StockPotImages.com

Principal photography © The Rev

Additional photographs by: Eli173, Gelston Dwight, Ian C., Mark Heinrich,
Malama Aina Seeds Hawaii, Monica Griffin, Ocanabis, Optimize Horticulture
Consulting, SnowHigh.

This book contains information about illegal substances, specifically the plant
Cannabis and its derivative products. Green Candy Press would like to emphasize
that Cannabis is a controlled substance in North America and throughout much
of the world. As such, the use and cultivation of cannabis can carry heavy penal-
ties that may threaten an individual's liberty and livelihood.

The aim of the Publisher is to educate and entertain. Whatever the Publisher's
view on the validity of current legislation, we do not in any way condone the use
of prohibited substances.

Printed in China by Oceanic Graphic International

Sometimes Massively Distributed by P.G.W.

To my soul mate, Maureen Aiken, in gratitude for her constant support, and for the wonderful attitude that has made this book and most of the great things in my life possible. We have been together for 20 years now. Cheers Mo, I hope we make it another 20 years. So much love.

Contents

Foreword

"True teachers are those who use themselves as bridges over which they invite their students to cross; then, having facilitated their crossing, joyfully collapse, encouraging them to create their own."
— Nikos Kazantzakis

A lot has changed since the man we know as the Rev released his first book, *True Living Organics: The Ultimate Guide to Growing All-Natural Marijuana Indoors*. Although readers of *SKUNK Magazine* were familiar with the Rev's methods and teaching for nearly five years, they and others thirsty for the same type of knowledge were finally able to access and understand a revolutionary idea all in one place. And they did, in significant numbers, as the book was incredibly well received and now stands as the go to manual for proponents of the organic way of life and growing.

The Rev touched the right nerve at exactly the right time as the book also represented a peaceful polemic manifesto on behalf of those who were tired of living in an artificial world where speed and mediocrity took precedence over quality and sustainability. We now recognize that cannabis is an effective medicine for a multitude of ailments. The Rev made us recognize that the best results only occurred when we paid as much attention as possible to what we were putting into our medicine, and by extension our bodies.

The Rev taught that there was a better way to grow: cleaner, cheaper, and with respect for the Earth's finite resources. This little book not only signaled a change in consciousness among growers but also more importantly, mirrored the changes happening within society. People are tired of seeing their waters polluted, their air dirty and their food poisoned. People are tired of being lied to by those who feign protection but are truly interested in profits and power. They have a friend and champion in the Rev.

Now, a few years later, the Rev's teachings are being put into practice more than ever before, from small closet growers, all the way to some of the largest outdoor grows in California. One dispensary in Colorado even offers their clients only TLO grown medicine, and their gardens operate with the Rev's principles at heart and in mind, only on a much larger scale.

With legalization that promises to change society on our doorstep, the Rev's philosophy is even more important as different factions vie for control of the plant and the way it will be grown. Synthetic nutrients, chemical pesticides, GMOs, and lack of husbandry have mired the way corporations produce many of the goods we consume, resulting in toxicity in both our bodies and our lands and waters. TLO is not simply a reaction to this, it is a call to go back to when nature functioned best, when it was unencumbered by influences trying to control it by altering the way she functioned. This book is important.

The Rev will likely turn a deep shade of Panama Red when he sees the way I describe him and his writings as he has remained humble throughout his successes and still retains his awe when learning more about cannabis. If I had to pick one thing to admire about him, it would be the absence of dogma within his preaching. Sure there are sacred tenets contained within his method, but he is always willing to listen, and sometimes reverse himself if presented with a better way. That is what makes him the Rev, and what makes it a privilege to have worked by his side for nearly a decade.

Thanks amigo,
John Vergados
Editor In Chief
SKUNK Magazine

Introduction

Greetings everyone! Welcome to this, the revised edition of True Living Organics. I thought it was important to update some of the information in this book and to pass on new knowledge; good stuff Maynard. Below, you'll find a ten-point list to better help you wrap your head around my TLO supernatural growing philosophy.

My soil and recycling recipes have evolved quite a bit in the years since this book was first published. You'll find new revised recipes in this edition. One huge goal when growing cannabis, any style, has always been dialing in the least amount of additions (food) while still maintaining the genetic potential of the plants. This new revised edition reflects that philosophy exactly, and although you can make these mixes stronger, you will likely have no need to. If for any reason you judge your soil mix to be too powerful, simply add 10-15% more bagged or recycled soil to the base mix. If you find it not strong enough then just make it the next time with 3 cubic feet of bagged or recycled soil mix rather than 3.5 cubic feet; easy, right? Whenever changing a living soil, use small steps.

All the recipes in this book have been thoroughly tested by me for years. Rather than give you ten tea recipes, I have given you three great recipes for teas. Feel free to adjust these all you want, once you understand the TLO way and have some working knowledge of what brings what to your teas. This way I have made things much easier to follow along with and minimized confusion—I thought the original edition of my book was a tad unorganized and have attempted to fix it, and I think I have. I've also simplified the section with spikes too. You'll see. Now, on with the show!

The 10 Commandments of TLO Container Growing

1. Cooking, or in other words composting, your recycled or custom soil mixes is essential to the whole TLO philosophy. Make sure you are doing this step well and pay special attention to it farther along in the book. During the cooking process we are processing most of the

amendments and organic matter into bonded up versions of themselves, and a ton of nutrients are temporarily immobilized in the massive populations of microlife that are always busy in any supernatural TLO living soil mix. This allows the living plants' roots (symbiotically working with those massive populations of microbes) to un-bond these nutrient elements as the plants need them. These elements include calcium, magnesium, iron, phosphorus, nitrogen, etc. You want your living soil mix to be uber alive and *well-cooked*, so make sure cooking is done thoroughly and don't rush it.

2. Soil and root temperatures in containers are elevated in comparison to plants in the ground, and when using the TLO growing style in containers we harness this enhanced metabolism. We do this by growing indoors, in warm outdoor locations or in outdoor greenhouses that are kept warm, by providing a lot of available water, food and air to all the life and microbeasties living in those containers. Another thing that is true under the enhanced metabolic conditions of container growing with TLO is that stated nutrient activation times are accelerated, and their length of activation is decreased. Things like blood meal and guanos will all be available to the plant faster than "usual" and something like a top dressing starts to help the plant in about 7-10 days. Things like the nitrogen in blood meal only last for about two months maximum in TLO containers, as opposed to the usual time of several months. Keep this in mind. In nature, most things move in about 10-14 day cycles—and it's the same with TLO. Patience is a virtue, Grasshopper.

3. By using the TLO system, we work with nature and play into her strengths as opposed to fighting her, which is, to my mind, what synthetic growing is all about. Most growers who pour liquid nutrients on their plants are unaware of how good cannabis plants, and likely all plants, are at taking care of their own needs and issues (when healthy and happy). All you need to do is stop trying to "fix" any small issue you may see by adding something besides good water. All the nutrients needed by the plant are in the TLO soil mix, so have no fear and remember it takes a plant about 10-15 days to fix any small problems herself, using her own abilities and (supernatural) resources. As you dive deeper into the TLO philosophy you will start to see all natural things making perfect sense with other all natural things.

4. The TLO philosophy is specific to container growing and living soil mixes. However, this is not to say that many aspects of TLO can't be

used outdoors in the ground via raised beds or spots composted upon; you can still use things like spikes, top dressings and teas to keep outdoor growing all natural, and you will just be taking it up a few notches with the TLO tweaks. Let me say for the record here that the very best way to utilize the TLO philosophy outdoors, when growing in the ground, is to use a top-down approach; simply composting on a spot for a whole season before you use it to plant in will do astounding things! Raised beds are primo for starting faster and you can certainly fill the raised beds with my Supernatural Soil Mix Recipe 2.2 or Recycling Soil Mix Recipe—just make sure it is cooked properly before exposing living roots to it (and use a chlorine/chloramine-free water source) or you will kick your own ass before you really get started.

5. You will quickly gain the skills to recognize über-happy plants as opposed to kind-of-happy plants once you have seen all your plants supernaturally happy using these methods. Your troubleshooting skills will also go through the roof and you will "see" things very early, allowing you to be 90% sure of what to do; or, more importantly what *not* to do. Most issues simply need a supply of good water and a good (low stress) environment. I will show you many of these common issues in pictures later in this book. As you tweak TLO to your own environment, do it slowly; often it takes months to see the good or bad effects from a new addition, or the removal of one. So my advice here is change things slowly, and only one thing at a time, until you see what you see. An example of this: If you start using brick coir products in your soil mix and worm farm, the intense levels of salts catch up to your soil mix about two months later; in my experience. But you should be able to see the good effects of things like top dressings or spike alterations much faster, within 10-15 days usually. I judge how healthy my soil mix is by how healthy my worms look when I see them, as they ride (alive) through my entire recycling process. Beautiful TLO-type soil mixes can vary quite a bit, as they just need diversity to cover all your bases. Start with my recommendations, and work your way from there; you owe it to yourself to do this properly because you need to SEE what this can do. In the words of Ron Swanson: "Don't half-ass two things. Whole-ass one thing."

6. With TLO you will flower high-yielding plants, of larger size overall, in smaller sized containers. This is one of the really superb aspects of TLO growing, and one that I prize dearly! I'm pretty old these days mis amigos, and I have a messed up leg too, so it's hard for me to lug around large containers with plants in them. Most organic container growing methods require you to use very large containers to achieve

Recycle everything in your TLO garden!

high-yielding plants, and I do mean LARGE! Using the uber-powerful TLO soil mix in conjunction with the spikes and layers, teas and top dressing, will really show you what a 2.5 gallon pot growing a 3 foot plant can do under a standard 400 (HID) watt bulb; even under 1,000 watt bulbs you only need 3.5 gallon pots to grow high yielding 5-6 foot plants. Of course genetics play a role here, but if your genetics have the potential to yield huge, you better believe they *will* when you employ TLO methods. Remember in order to get bigger yields, it's way more important what you don't do, or don't add—*you savvy?*

7. No force feeding! Now this one is a huge biggie my green friends, and one of the colossal departures from everything you have likely been taught about growing cannabis by corporations. We DO NOT pour ANY liquid fertilizers—organic or otherwise—on to our plants or soil—ever! Only teas should be used for additional nutrition when needed, and we

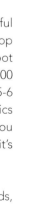

never force feed (chelate) by using liquids containing high levels of organic acids like humic, fulvic, ascorbic, citric and phosphoric acids to name several of the culprits. All these acids are good, and chelation is how the plant feeds from the soil, but the key is to let the microlife handle all the chelating at normal, all natural levels and not to supplement these acids, otherwise you will at the very least disturb the microbial life, inhibiting their abilities to cause supernatural growth. You can screw up a fantastic TLO grow by thinking that if you add just a little fertilizer it will add to your harvest quality and size. It will *not*, so don't do it.

8. Just add (good) water! Make SURE you understand what *good* water is, as defined in this book, and then see to it that your water is up to these standards—or as close as can be. If your water is not *consistently* good water, your chances of experiencing the supernatural results of TLO are low. Most well water and city tap water is horrible water for container growing in living soil, and I will explain this in more detail further along in this book. If you want to use slightly larger pots to flower in than I do, with spikes and layers, you can literally just add good water for your whole grow—seriously, I have done it many times!

9. Recycle everything! TLO growing is an almost totally self-sustaining style. We recycle roots and extra plant matter like leaves and stems as well as our soil. TLO soil mix is like a fine wine and, when done correctly, only gets better with age. At the time of writing the soil mix I use is going on six years old, I shit you not. Recycling our soil not only saves us money, it also allows us to play to Mother Nature's natural strengths. The microbial life in the living soil evolves very quickly, and within just a couple months your microlife will have started to evolve into YOUR particular environment to a huge degree, and they continue to evolve, getting better and better at their jobs (in your specific gardening environment) as time goes on. You'll see!

10. Follow my recommendations as closely as you can and don't try and apply your own knowledge of growing to my recommendations unless you are *very* savvy regarding all natural elemental sources and composition. This way you can truly see what TLO can do;. These are all formulas that I have personally tested and retested for over a decade now, and that's out of the 40 years that I have been growing cannabis. Seriously, have a little faith baby, have a little faith; it will pay off big time.

We are going to take a three-pronged approach in this book. I will give you recipes for your first TLO soil mix, and for your recycling soil mix, as well as awesome cannabis growing enhancements for your earthworm farm if you choose to have one. You don't need a worm farm, but I highly recommend it; you will however, need some earthworm castings or primo compost. You only need to use the Supernatural Soil Mix Recipe 2.2 the first time when you start with bagged soil, and then we recycle it all over and over and over. My soil is six years old and 100% recycled. It's a beautiful thing.

A Few Overdue Words of Thanks

I want to thank SKUNK Magazine, especially Attilio, John and Niko. Working with all of you has really been, and continues to be, such a pleasure. Thank you for everything. I likely would not be the author of this book if not for all the SKUNK love—*wink*.

I want to thank The Three Little Birds, GW Heyduke, Caligrower, RC Cola and Wodan, for helping to guide me along my chosen all natural path. Others are Dr. Elaine Ingham, who fed me a plethora of great knowledge regarding the living soil; Aeroman, who taught me how to REALLY grow well using aeroponics—even though I no longer practice those skills, it was damn nice of him to share such valuable knowledge with me; and KQ, a mystery man from long ago, who one time in a forum post told me that one day I would change the accepted cannabis paradigm. I hope you were correct my good man, because that couldn't be more spot on as my goal.

Thanks to NDNGuy, Tokestar, Dr. Smitty, Zoltron, GW Heyduke, Mo-Holes, Forehead, AB Normal and many others for sourcing awesome genetics for me; you guys rock! I know I have forgotten so many of you because there are many more; you dorks were some of my favorite online friends. Cheers! Special shout out to my buddy Happydaze, who inspires me in unique ways—thank you man, you have helped me more than you know.

Big thanks also to my publisher, Green Candy Press—Andrew, Jack and Heather ("The Crispy Betty")—who have all been great to work with since day one. Thank you all so much.

Here are a few links for you:
Get your KOS genetics at: kingdomorganicseeds.com
Friend me (The Rev) on Facebook at: Michael Paige
Like KOS on Facebook at: Kingdom Organic Seeds
Like Skunk Magazine on Facebook at: SKUNK Magazine
Like TLO Book on Facebook at: True Living Organics

TLO SOIL MIX SALTY DOG'S GUIDE

You are always doing a balancing act when growing all-naturally, so when you are TLO growing you are growing in a soil blend with a high content of salts; so let's not just assume "salts" are bad, some are, but the ones in my soil recipes are balanced for high performance in optimal warm conditions under intense lighting. Should your conditions be less high performance you could benefit from making the soil recipes weaker. You also don't need (or want) to use large container sizes relative to plant size, because those heavy salts are really heavy nutrients, mostly locked up via "cooking" the soil mix, but still, it's plenty for the plant and the massive microbial populations in those containers.

Here are a few guidelines:

• If your temperature at your plants' tops doesn't get above 85°F very often, and/or you don't use intense lighting, then you can easily cut the strength of the soil recipes by 1/3rd (up to ½) with bagged soil or compost. 2 parts TLO soil blend, to 1 part bagged soil/compost. Then when recycling just use 1/3rd less additions than recommended in my recipes.

• Only "pure" water (20 PPM or less) should be used with all these suggested recipes; however, if you have to use water higher in PPM values with calcium and magnesium, you must dial down your additions of dolomite lime (oyster shells and bone meal as well). I would start with a 20% reduction across the board with those elements I listed and see what you see. It's a balancing act; remember that ground water often changes in PPM value from season to season. So "pure" water here is worth the hassle for stability's sake.

• Try to not think along the lines of adding something like Silica Blast for silicon additions, or various liquid "nectar" products that are rife with humic and/or fulvic acids and often other organic acids. This is not TLO supernatural style. The recipes in this book are truly sustainable with just good "pure" water, period. These types of liquid growing products cause an environmental hurricane for the microbeasties, which keeps them from doing what they do best. Just take care of your soil, and make your environment as cannabis friendly as possible and observe—you dig?

This beauty is TLO-grown in Hawaii by Malama Aina Seeds

- My soil blends in this book are highly unconventional; literally, you simply must refrain from the constant need to add some new liquid element to a TLO garden. There's plenty of food in these soil mixes, that's why they work so well in smaller containers using just "pure" water 90% of the time. Seriously, just add water! A stable environment that allows your massively reproducing and evolving microlife to go Supernatural is what you are after here, Jedi.

CHAPTER 1

What is True Living Organics?

TLO growth is super natural

The concept of True Living Organics (TLO) is not something I invented—not at all. Instead, I recognized some of the natural processes at work and worked hard to optimize them further and further. Subse-

Hash made from TLO buds will almost literally blow your mind

quently, I coined the term True Living Organics as a "supernatural" growing style, which focuses greatly upon the soil life, and specifically the microbial life within that soil.

Within this book, I'm going to assume that you have a certain level of knowledge about growing marijuana. This book is intended as a complete guide to TLO growing rather than a beginner's guide to growing cannabis. There are some fantastic beginner's grow books out there, such as Greg Green's *Cannabis Grow Bible,* and if you've never grown before I recommend reading one of these guides in conjunction with this book. If you have grown marijuana before and understand the simple processes involved, like a proper environment, you'll have no problem grasping the concepts behind TLO growing, the great rewards and the practicalities of changing your grow to a TLO set up.

Way before man ever walked on planet Earth, plants evolved and came out of the seas and onto the land. This was only possible thanks to the symbiotic relationship the plants have with fungi, bacteria, protozoa and many other types of microbial life. This microlife, in turn, supports a food chain—which is really better described as a food web—that helps feed the plants. Be sure to check out my further reading recommendations to expand your mind in relation to these subjects.

So What Exactly is True Living Organics?

TLO is an all natural/organic style of growing in which the power is given BACK to the plant. For more time than we can understand, plants have been feeding their own needs by finding what they require in the soil in which they live. Cannabis has always done the same. Somewhere along the line, cannabis growers started taking the decisions away from the plant, and after that, they even took away the soil. They force fed their plants with nutrients even when they didn't want them. They took away the natural sources of elements and replaced them with synthetics. And I should know; I was one of those growers that suffered at their greedy hands, but thought I was kicking ass.

Now, though, I'm doing things differently. My True Living Organics style is a world away from nutrient solutions and chemical additives. TLO growing uses the power of the microlife to let the plant feed itself what it needs, when it needs it. It puts the plant in charge of itself rather than at the mercy of the grower, or of what the Hydro shop guy says to do. You see, a plant's roots actually communicate with the microlife that live underground in the area immediately surrounding the roots (the rhizosphere). The plant offers up certain elements that attract the appropriate microlife. These microlife create nutrients that the plant requires, and bringing them close means that these nutrients are then available to the plant. The activity of all the microbeasties creates all natural and organic chelating acids and compounds. This is the main process that we don't want to upset by adding unnaturally chelated liquids, lest those microguys die from atrophy. This delicate

REV'S TIP Soil made for cannabis in containers has to be much different than soil(s) made for other plants, due to cannabis' voracious appetite and growth rates, especially under typical high performance grow room conditions. The rules are different for high temp high metabolism soil and the amount of life you will be feeding (the microbeasties); so, hells yes TLO soil mixes are strong; there's a lot of life besides the plant chowing down (consuming nutrients).

This TLO-grown plant is of connoisseur quality

These buds are TLO-grown Shadow Haze from
my own Kingdom Organic Seeds

symbiosis can be totally messed up by doing something as simple as adding liquid nutrients that are chelated using organic acids; they're all organic for sure, but not suitable for TLO growing. By using such products, you will devastate the microbial population into a chaotic state, and to avoid being too technical, we'll just say that this has the same effect on the microlife as the bends has on SCUBA divers who come up too fast. In chaos, the microlife is not nearly as helpful to the plant roots, and if the pH swings too far it can actually kill the majority of the microlife. It should go without saying that micro-genocide is not good for your plant. Fungi can sustain a harder pH hit and any pH dive will certainly favor the fungi bouncing back first, which is not as cool as it sounds—containers dominated by fungi very often drop to deadly low pH levels, too low for cannabis plants to survive in.

In TLO growing, the soil mix we use is literally alive, no joke. Much like the delicate balance of life on Earth in, say, the African plains, there is a delicate dynamic in your container's soil mix. There are the big guys who throw their weight around (the lions and the zebras of your soil) and the little guys who aren't as obvious but are just as important (like those all-important bees). TLO shows you how to bring in and harness all of these microbeasties to work for you. I've never had higher quality cannabis than the stuff I get from a TLO harvest, and I am a 40-year veteran grower/smoker, so, as you can imagine, I've smoked some cannabis in my time. In addition, all the most impressive genetic traits of different cannabis varieties really stand out in TLO, and the aromas, flavors, high-type and colors for which we choose any particular plant are all made that little more amazing. It is the best of the best for smoking, especially for the medical and connoisseur communities.

What TLO doesn't include is synthetically chelated nutrients, most pesticides, and many fungicides. It does not include heavy chelation (force feeding) of nutrients with the use of liquid ascorbic, fulvic and humic acids at all. Instead, organic teas are "brewed" and in this process, the amount of microbial life increases dramatically. Such teas are applied to the plants once a month, or more often if you choose; I use them about once or twice a month myself. This helps to bring in life that, if we were growing outdoors, would already be in the soil, but because we're growing in containers, we want to provide for the plant. Once the tea is applied, all the microlife goes to work processing organic matter and breaking down mineral elements in the container soil mix, as well as distributing the already broken down nutrient elements in the tea. Make no mistake, your plant containers are their own little universes and are always teeming with life.

REV'S TIP Chelating nutrients is a pretty straightforward process, and to spare you a lot of technobabble, it basically means you can encase/combine nutrients within the chelating elements, which are then easily (or rather, forcefully) absorbed by the roots of plants, along with any nutrients trapped within. Chelating goes way beyond our purposes here in this book, but suffice it to say that we want natural chelates from the microlife to work for us and our plants. We do not force feed through excessive chelation using the TLO style, because it isn't natural, and only serves to piss off or kill the microlife that TLO soil relies upon and will result in an inferior final product regarding yields and potency, in my experience.

TLO growing can almost be considered a "just add water" growing style. Rather than buying and using pre-made mixes, in TLO growing you prepare the soil mix yourself. This allows the container soil mix environment to stay relatively the same over time as far as pH and nutrient levels/ratios are concerned, and this in turn is conducive to the microbial life and allows them to reach the equilibrium of a delicate and balanced soil food web. As mentioned above, this is much like the food chain/web of the African plains in many ways. This has several added benefits for the grower: You don't have to worry about adding liquid nutrients with every (any) watering, and you don't need to concern yourself with balancing the pH of your water, or anything else, as long as the water you use is of good quality. In fact, as a TLO grower, your primary objective is to take good care of the soil life so the soil life will take very good care of your plants.

Growing a little team of indoor TLO plants

Learning to grow your cannabis TLO style will most likely result in you growing the finest top-shelf marijuana that you will ever cultivate. At first your yields might be lower, but don't worry. By applying some of the techniques that I will show you, you can increase your yields over a little bit of time. It can be difficult for some people to lose *the synthetic mindset* of using liquid nutrients to force feed their plants, but I ask that you try. Your yields and quality can both be much higher if you refrain from pouring on anything except an organic tea a couple of times a month. In my experience, getting bigger and better yields is all about getting a perfectly balanced soil mix, and the simple addition of good water, along with choosing not to do many things. TLO is a lot about what's *not* in it.

The 'L' in TLO stands for Living. Like these love bugs!

What you learn here, when applied, will result in both a gift and a curse. You will actually experience smoking totally natural cannabis, maybe for the first time in your life. Many of you think you have already done this, but in reality you most likely have not, unless you are or you know an old school outdoor grower who is savvy with all natural ways. Once you see how elegant and smooth naturally grown herb can be, you will never look back.

Just one more note: Get over any phobias to "bugs" you have right now. The *L* in TLO stands for Living, and I'm not kidding around. When you look at your soil mix closely, it should move. You know you have achieved Druid Status in TLO growing when you can recycle your soil and have it work primo—and when you find suddenly that your product is the one everyone wants most because it's the best there is. A hard-grained synthetic mindset can be difficult to overcome, but it's important to remember that pouring unnatural liquid food onto your plants is not what TLO is about at all. Keep trying to lose that mindset; be tenacious, and you will prevail!

You can find out all about TLO in the following pages, and I want to keep this book as trim as possible, so let's get cracking, yeah?

ALL THE ELEMENTS CANNABIS REQUIRES

None of these elements are in reality more important than the others. Nutrient elements are like everything else in nature's design; they all work together. Try and avoid the whole perception that there is some kind of "magic bullet" within special nutrients only, because they are all important. Another important aspect of TLO growing is never forgetting about the living soil microbeasties. They require all these same elements themselves, especially oxygen, nitrogen, and calcium in my experience.

Carbon and oxygen are absorbed from the air, while other nutrients including water are obtained from the soil. Plants must obtain the following mineral nutrients from the growing media:

- **Primary Macronutrients:** nitrogen (N), phosphorus (P), potassium (K)
- **Secondary Macronutrients:** calcium (Ca), sulfur (S), magnesium (Mg)
- **The Macronutrient:** Silicon (Si)
- **Micronutrients:** boron (B), chlorine (Cl), manganese (Mn), iron (Fe), zinc (Zn), copper (Cu), molybdenum (Mo), nickel (Ni), selenium (Se), and sodium (Na)

CARBON
Carbon forms the backbone of many plants bio-molecules, including starches and cellulose. Carbon is fixed through photosynthesis from the carbon dioxide in the air and is a part of the carbohydrates that store energy in the plant.

HYDROGEN
Hydrogen also is necessary for building sugars and building the plant. It is obtained almost entirely from water. Hydrogen ions are imperative for a proton gradient to help drive the electron transport chain in photosynthesis and for respiration.

OXYGEN
Oxygen is necessary for cellular respiration. Cellular respiration is the process of generating energy-rich **adenosine triphosphate** (ATP) via the consumption of sugars made in photosynthesis. Plants produce oxygen gas during photosynthesis to produce glucose, but then require oxygen to break down this glucose.

CHAPTER 2

Preparing Your Grow Space

I love grow tents for my personal gardens

If this is your first TLO grow, you will most likely need to change the style or layout of your grow area somewhat, just as you'll have to change your mindset. Your basic environment for TLO is broad; the same rules that apply to all natural/organic growing also apply to TLO growing. I myself have grown with TLO using many different environmental styles, in very different sized spaces. TLO growing is very flexible, and can be adapted into both small and larger outdoor grows, as well as almost any size of indoor grow. For this book, we'll stick to the indoors environment, and I will suggest recipes and whatnot on smaller scales for most of you newer medical and connoisseur growers, who want to grow, and use, the highest quality medicine possible. To up the scale of your garden, simply do a little math, and you can increase the ratios to any level you like. See my writings later in this book regarding teas on a larger scale, as special rules apply here.

Here's a little note regarding your grow area. A while ago I moved from a very large space out in the east county in southern Oregon. Now I am confined to one 8 x 8 x 8-foot bedroom and part of a small garage, and two external smaller tents. I use the garage to store and mix my bulk soils and do my recycling, and I root clones and keep males in the two external tents. I have pulled the whole enchilada off in just one bedroom before, recycling and all, without a single problem. Don't let the restrictions of your grow area put you off TLO growing. Where there's a will, there's a way.

I know some of you will want to go large scale right out of the gate with TLO, and while that's fine, I recommend you learn the skills of

TLO growing first, as this will save you vast amounts of work—and money. Understanding how the all natural world of growing plants actually works will add massively to your understanding of how easily it works on a big scale—without a ton of work or a ton of money. Once you have your soil recycling handled and it is working great, you will be ready to go bigger if you like. If you are already growing and depending upon harvesting plants using other methods like synthetics, just take a few plants and run them TLO style. I will give you a fast soil mix later in this book so you can give a few plants a TLO test drive without putting your whole garden on the line.

Lighting Options for TLO Indoors

Although much of the TLO growing technique is different to ones that you might have used before, the basics are still the same. No matter what situation they're grown in, cannabis plants always need light, food and water, and lighting especially is a huge factor in growing the biggest and best buds possible—*duh*!

Good lighting makes a huge difference

LED Grow Hut

HIDs over the flowering chamber of a TLO grow

High-Intensity Discharge Lights (HIDs)

I'm going to be fairly straightforward about this: For lighting, I prefer using bulbs with better overall spectrums (close to that of the sun) for growing. One of my all time favorite bulbs for full term, sprout to harvest TLO growing is the Eye Blue Metal Halide (MH). My least favorite is the High Pressure Sodium (HPS) bulb. HPS bulbs do not seem to allow the plant to absorb and/or process nutrients as well as the Eye Blue MH bulbs, unless you are growing with a synthetic set up or a "soup style" organic set up, which I will discuss later in this book. The MH and HPS lights are both High-Intensity Discharge (HID) lights, which use a decent amount of electricity and create a lot of heat as well. Both these issues must be considered, in terms of both your wallet and the venting/air exchange in your grow room or grow tents. Generally, the heat can be dealt with by installing a small fan to cool the air directly under the light or by venting the lights directly. In my personal garden space I vent several tents within a single room and do not vent the lights directly; this simply means I must manually be present to open up the tents everyday when the lights come on. The cash flow problems aren't so easily solved! TLO is a bit of an investment out of the gate but gets really affordable as time goes on. During your first year of TLO growing look back on your expenses compared to your old way of doing things and I think you'll like what you see!

Don't try and save a few bucks by getting yourself some other brand of Blue Metal Halide bulbs amigos; you want the Eye Blue bulbs. I have tried many others and was always disappointed when compared to the results using the Eye Blue MH.

LEDs over a TLO vegetative room

Light Emitting Diode (LED)

LED grow lamps have come on leaps and bounds in recent years, and if you have issues with heat and high electricity bills, you may want to think about using LEDs for the vegetative growth stage at least. I used to laugh at the very concept of LED grow lights, but I now use them religiously as they seem to work great with TLO growing in the vegetative state. I have essentially replaced my 400 watt HID Blue MH bulbs with 205 watt LEDs for the vegetative stage, and the results are even better than they were previously. The growth is very stacked with über-short internodes.

Since the first edition of this book I have found several LED lights that will indeed flower well in TLO growing, but here's the rub where LEDs are concerned, in my experience: First of all the spectrum must be considered, and spectral ranges down in the yellow/red spectrum are the most common types with LEDs. I would recommend a high-quality LED first of all, with a great warranty from a manufacturer who has been in the biz awhile. Second thing I would want is a spectrum up around 5500 K (Kelvin) for vegging and for flowering; we are growing all naturally here and the sunshine doesn't change spectrum much during flowering season, you dig? You *can* use the more red/yellow spectra of LEDs full term, or just for flowering, but I prefer the fuller spectrum LEDs for maximum yields and resin production.

Fluorescent and Compact Fluorescent Lighting (CFL)

These bulbs have their place in any indoor grow room. I tend to root cuttings under small 21 watt blue CFL bulbs from General Electrics (GE), and I always like to keep freshly planted cuttings, as well as mother and father clones, under fluorescent lighting (T5s) too. For

LED lighting works great using quality LED lights

TLO garden growing beautifully under HIDs

these purposes I also tend to favor the bluer or "cooler" bulb spectra that are sometimes referred to as daylight bulbs as well, as I believe it helps the plants to grow roots faster than the redder or "warmer" spectrum. Under these light sources, the plant's metabolism will be slower than under HID lights, which is why they are ideal for longer-term clones that you don't want growing particularly quickly.

I like to keep long-term clones under fluorescents or LEDs under cooler temperatures than grow room temps. If these weaker LED/fluorescent lights are used within an already warm grow room, you can get rapid (leggy) growth expressions. It's nice to have a tent you can place in another room or garage here for this purpose—really a great idea for breeders—and you don't need any fancy venting on these along with your power usage being über-low. For these types of tents (long-term mother/father clones) my temps never drop below say mid 50s (Fahrenheit) and never really top the upper 70s. Have a small fan for circulation and the top/roof vent open on the tent. Open a lower vent for cool air to enter and boom! Your tent will thermally vent from the warm air inside rising out through the top, and in these cooler temps with less intense lighting they will thrive—a bit slower, is all.

PHOTO: IAN C.

REV'S TIP   In my experience, HID lights are NOT a good choice for rooting cuttings.

> **REV'S TIP** The true Supernatural TLO way: If you sometimes have big fears of losing a precious elite clone, just get at least two separate cloners, like smaller Clone King Cloners, and split your clones up between them. This way, if one cloner develops any problems (like a pump fail etc.) you still have some of the valuable cuts in the other one. The bottom line is clones work better in containers and seed plants work better outdoors in the ground. This is seriously true in my experience.

Sprouting and vegging under HID and LED bulbs will really increase your growth rates and add to your yields at the end as well. I recommend Eye Blue Halides for these purposes, depending on your specific needs with regards to heat and power bills. I also love the newer LEDs for the vegetative growth stage, and some work very impressively for the flowering stage too. Some of these LEDs seem to almost equal the performance of HID lights, despite the HID lights being twice the wattage of the LEDs in some cases. For rooting cuttings in an aero cloner or bubble rooter, I like the smaller 21 watt CFL bulbs from GE or cool fluorescents, both kept at a height of approximately 1-2 feet from the tops of the cuttings.

Cloning for TLO

There are almost as many ways to clone as there are ways to grow cannabis. I personally am a huge fan of the aeroponic and bubble cloner methods. My friends have cloned in peat pots (Jiffy Pots) successfully, and I have successfully used perlite and vermiculite as well as rockwool many times in the past. I never have needed any gels, rooting hormones or anything else apart from straight-up tap water or R/O filtered water. This applies to aero, bubble and all other forms of cloning I know of. Don't believe the hype, *mi amigos;* all you need here is aerated water that is not too high in dissolved salts and has no nitrogen added!

My favorite cloning bulb

Rooting cannabis cuttings is fairly straightforward, and there is a ton of good information all over the internet and in the many growing books out there. I would recommend Greg Green's *Cannabis Grow Bible* for all general advice on growing that is not covered in this book, including how to root cuttings. However, I will tell you this: You should always try to take your cuttings from the lower branches if possible. How fast your cuttings will root is largely relative to how much nitrogen is being stored in that cutting, *and* how healthy that branch is. Since nitrogen is a mobile nutrient (meaning it can freely move around in the plant to wherever it is most needed) it would be available in higher concentrations at the growing tip (or tips) of the plant, closest to the lights. Some strains also tend to root much more easily than others, so take this into account as well.

On a dry erase board (The Cloner Board), you simply draw your template of clone locations using a Sharpie or other hardcore permanent marker. After that, you just use normal dry erase pens to label the cuttings in their locations and just erase them after they come out rooted. This Cloner Board is for labeling cuttings in a 36 site Clone King Cloner and keeps things organized in a busy garden with many varieties.

I am still using an aero cloner these days, and I have changed it up just a little bit. I use pure reverse osmosis filtered water (distilled or rain water would work just as well) in my cloner now with a little CaMg+ added at a ratio of about five drops per gallon of water. I get rooted clones faster than when I use just tap water by about three days and my roots are much healthier. Also, remember that the plant is quite capable of manufacturing its own rooting hormones and you never need to add anything like this to your cuttings, ever. Seriously, don't buy into the synthetic hyped mindset.

Aero cloning is the way

Old school rockwool cloning works fine too

Other TLO Grow Room Considerations

Temperature and Humidity are always concerns when growing cannabis and this is no different when growing TLO style. Indoors, a general rule of thumb for the desired temperature *at the plant tops* is around mid to high 80s (F) when lights are on, and mid–high 60s (F) when lights are off. Humidity should be around 50% or higher during lights off and 40–60% during lights on, optimally. Your grow room may be at mid 70s or whatever, but the most important temperature readings will be right where the plant tops are, under the lights. In this exact area you don't want the plant tops to exceed about 86°F for too long, and not by much. I normally dial everything in so my plant tops are at about 80-85°F during lights on, and this is primo.

REV'S TIP Best aero-cloner water ever is simply pure water with 10 drops of CaMg+ per gallon—Boom! Using a small (adjustable & accurate) aquarium water heater (under 100 watts) in your aero-cloners and keeping water temps around 68°F will really help out a ton when your cloner runs in cooler ambient temps.

Dehumidifiers and Humidifiers can both be used to your advantage in TLO growing, depending on your particular needs. Portable air-conditioning units are also great in the right circumstances. If your plants become infected by mildew or mold, then you will need to keep your grow room as dry as possible. If you also have spider mites, they happen to love a dry environment, and will flourish especially quickly in dry and hot conditions. If your grow rooms are free from parasitic molds, insects and arthropods, like they should be (and I will tell you how to achieve this in this book), then you can actually run higher humidity levels, which benefits the plants in several ways. Sustained low humidity will often result in potassium (K) issues, to give just one example.

Never aim the output of a dehumidifier or A/C unit directly at plants. I never need a dehumidifier these days, but if I run my Eye Blue

TLO roots growing well in aeroponics

halide lights during the summer months I do employ a portable A/C unit to keep the room within the ranges I have stated above for temps. My humidity is always around 40-60% with no worries. Take note that both portable A/C units and de-humidifiers both draw some serious power/amps and A/C units need an out vent as well for hot air, and dehumidifiers normally require a drain hose or reservoir to hold air-collected water.

The cloner board

Venting and CO₂ are two of the most ignored and/or misunderstood facets of grow room environmental tweaking. In TLO, dealing with these is real easy. Make sure to have some decent venting (air exchange) and that will handle the CO_2 needs of the plants as well. Raising CO_2 levels artificially, with CO_2 tanks, is fine if you really want to, but be sure to go super duper mellow. Just make sure you handle your exhaust venting. This will, in turn, handle several potential problems, like humidity, heat and CO_2. Allow for passive intake, and if you intake from outside, use a screen or nylon stocking as a filter to keep unwanted pests outside.

I DO NOT RECOMMEND raising your CO_2 levels artificially; this can be detrimental to an indoor TLO garden. This strategy is better suited for hydroponics grows using synthetic nutrients—seriously!

REV'S TIP As always, when running any electrical equipment in your garden, you want to make sure there are no errant LEDs on during lights out in the flowering period, or else hermaphrodites will result. Hermaphrodites will ruin your sinsemilla harvest by pollinating your plants. Some LEDs can be found on humidifiers and other electrical equipment, so be sure to stand in your grow room during lights off and look for any stray sources of light. Electrical tape works pretty well to cover some of these up, and if you get older style dehumidifiers, humidifiers, heaters, A/C units, etc, they normally have no lights. Notorious LED hiding places are power strips and surge suppressors, along with digital timers and portable heaters. The red glow of any space heater also counts as light here.

REV'S TIP Ambient temperatures of your garden can make huge differences in your plants' nutrient getting abilities via the microlife. This is because the microbeasties really work best, in my opinion (in containers), once the soil temperatures are above 75°F – this means your garden ambient temps are up around mid/high 80's.

OMRI label means
good to go in TLO

Some pseudo organic
growing supplies

Organic Styles of Growing

Pseudo Organic—or "Mostly Organic"—Growing Styles are the same as synthetic growing styles, as far as the quality of the results goes. Products that are "Organic Based" or ones that do not say that they contain "All" or "100%" all natural/organic ingredients fall into this category, as does all of the Botanicare line. All Botanicare products have some degree of chelating with synthetic salts. Fox Farm's Tiger Bloom is another one with synthetics, and it reads "Organic Based" on the label. Botanicare's Organicare line of liquid organic nutrients are probably organic, but better suited for "soup style" growing than TLO growing.

If you ever hear anybody tell you that well-flushed synthetic cannabis is as smooth smoking as all natural/organic cannabis, it is because they have never actually smoked true organically grown cannabis. In reality, the two are not even close. I am an expert at hydro-synthetic indoor growing, and used this style for easily a decade before turning to TLO, so I know the difference. Even a very small amount of synthetic food makes your smoke go from A+++ to ordinary, and if you pull off a TLO harvest done well, you will be a true believer too. Synthetic herb sucks compared to all natural/organic herb. The two are as different as night and day.

"Soup Style" Organic Growing means simply to rely on organic liquid nutrients from bottles as your main food source. Many types of these liquid nutrients are chelated heavily with all natural organic acids, like humic, fulvic, phosphoric and ascorbic acids, to name just four of them. As long as you stay absolutely organic/all natural with your liquids, your buds will come out way better than any synthetic style of growing, as far as flavors, smells and smoothness of smoking are concerned. However, "soup style" growing will not give you the great results that TLO growing gives, in my humble opinion, and there is a significant difference in aromatics and potency, which I think are greatly enhanced in TLO growing. In TLO we do not force feed the plant with large amounts of chelating organic acids—*amen*.

Strategies for Choosing All Natural Nutrients

When it comes to choosing your nutrients, I would normally say read the labels thoroughly and carefully, and while this is always a great idea, it often still won't tell you what you really need to know. Marketing geniuses are very good at their jobs, and in the nutrient industry this is especially true; making synthetic fertilizers *appear to be organic* is

> **REV'S TIP** Look for the OMRI label on any products you wish to use. OMRI stands for the Organic Materials Review Institute, and any product flying this label is (almost) always good to use in a TLO grow room or any true organic grow set up. If you don't see this label, you have to be a good investigator, because marketing geniuses are really good at making non-organic nutrients appear to be organic. What you should look for is whether it has any synthetic chelating salts in it or not, or high levels of organic acids. If it does, it sucks for TLO growing and for any true all natural growing style. If it is free from synthetic chelating salts and high levels of organic acids, then it gets the thumbs up. I don't use anything from a bottle these days except a little CaMg+ and molasses, period, and I highly recommend you do the same.

The aisle of death. Not a place you want to be!

child's play when most people don't understand what organic actually means. Call the manufacturers directly if you have doubts, and be direct with them. Ask them if they have any synthetic chelating elements in their fertilizer. Chelating is pronounced like *key-layting*, just so you sound serious. Always avoid products that use the term "Organic Based" because in my experience this almost always means that the product contains synthetic chelating salts, which are very bad. If you see the phrase "Made with organic or natural nutrients" be very wary too. The container for the product should state that the product is made with 100% or all natural or organic nutrients/elements. It also helps to have the OMRI tag on it clearly visible. OMRI stands for the Organics Materials Review Institute, and I need to add here also that organic acids are totally OMRI approved, so if you are purchasing liquid nutrients for some reason, like for your teas, make triple sure they are not full of organic acids. But you have no need for any liquid nutrients, and using most (like 99%) of them will not work out well for you.

With TLO growing you really never need any liquid nutrients and I only have about three on hand at any time. I'll list them below for you, with some info relating to why and when I use them.

REV'S TIP A fast, all natural liquid TLO friendly (all purpose) fertilizer is very simple: 1 teaspoon of liquid (Alaska brand) 5-1-1 N-P-K, and 2 teaspoons of liquid (Fox Farm brand) Big Bloom, per gallon of pure water. Don't use this one once the plant is 3.5 weeks from harvesting, or less.

Big Bloom! This is really the only liquid fertilizer I ever have available to me at home as I have gotten rid of all the rest. Big Bloom (by Fox Farm) is alright to use in teas and I like this nutrient as it is essentially an organic tea made with bat guano and earthworm castings, along with many other good things. Take note of the NPK (Nitrogen, Phosphorous and Potassium respectively) numbers, because they are very low in comparison to many liquid organic nutrients; this is a good thing. If need be, you could use this at a ratio of ¼ cup per gallon of bubbling tea water, but I use it in teas at a ratio of more like 2 tablespoons per gallon of bubbling tea, if and when I do use any. You should also be aware that this product contains decent levels of sodium chloride (sea salt) and as with all salty nutrients we don't want to be using so much of the Big Bloom that over time our salts build up in our living soil mix, causing big problems. If you decide to use it and it works well for your needs, use it sparingly.

CaMg+ is a calcium and magnesium liquid amendment I use for the sake of convenience and it works very well indeed. It is calcium and magnesium with a small dash of simple sugars. I always add it to my reverse osmosis filtered water at a rate of approximately 15 drops per gallon of water, bringing my PPM up to 60-80 on a TDS meter. If you can't get or don't want to use this product, no worries. Just cut your pure water with spring water to bring it up to the desired PPM level. See the Supernatural Soil Mix Recipe 2.2 later in this book for a way to adjust your soil mix so you don't need to add anything to your pure R/O, rain or distilled water.

I no longer use CaMg+ in my water; but, it is an option if you need to amend your Ca and/or Mg levels

Molasses is a mainstay for teas always. Just don't overdo it and stay within my recommendations because too much molasses will raise magnesium levels in your soil mix to an unhealthy level, and the top of your soil mix in your containers will become crusty. It won't absorb water quickly, and will suffocate plant roots. I use molasses at a rate of about 1 teaspoon per gallon (max, and usually less), and if you use teas rarely or often, 1 teaspoon per gallon is plenty.

For long-term storage of any natural liquid nutrients, like Big Bloom, use only cooler places. Often indoor grow room temperatures will cause liquid nutrients to spoil within a couple of months. If you ever pop the lid on one of your liquids and there is pressure release and/or a funky smell, toss it immediately!

Handling Pests Safely in TLO Indoor Gardens

This is, perhaps, the most important information to you in this book, so please read it carefully. There is a lot of really evil stuff out there that people use on their plants to get rid of mites, molds and other parasites. Often I hear this excuse for using dangerous chemicals: "It works really well!" Well, so would Raid and Roach Killer, but you wouldn't use that on your plants. Killing power is NOT the only factor when choosing a way to combat these little bastards in your TLO gardens. Avoid using Floramite and Avid like The Plague!

The Nuclear Option

If you are tired of always fighting mites and mold in a war you won't win in the end, why not just get some good seeds, then kill all your plants, or give them away? Keep all your garden space free from any living plants for 10 days and keep your garden space above 68°F during this time. Once the 10 days has passed, sprout some good genetics and find your favorite females to clone. Keep friends from coming into your garden if they have been in infected gardens recently, and don't come into your indoor garden directly after gardening outside; mites and mold spores are extremely good at hitchhiking, *believe* me!

I know many of you won't even consider doing this for various reasons, but it's a pro move that will make your growing experiences much better, and bigger, and it will cost you much less in money and time fighting the parasitic bastards. Do it right, then keep it clean. I am in the habit of doing everything I have to do in my gardens first thing after I wake up in the morning; that way I don't have to worry about where I have been lately, and it makes it easier for my old brain that way. The Nuclear Option is severe, but your grow room will be like the Garden of Eden afterwards.

The use of products like Avid and Floramite is not only a bad idea, it's also a dangerous one. Anytime you see something is meant for use on "ornamentals" then don't use it on food or smoke crops, ever! Hot

Mite and mold free plants yield much better

Shotz No Pest Strips are also bad to have around, and I see these in far too many grow rooms. It's like slowly spraying Raid on your plants, and anytime you see a warning about having a product around animals and humans (like the warning on the Hot Shotz label) then you can pretty safely assume it's not good around food or smoke crops. It's far worse than you likely think regarding these and their toxic potential, so don't do it.

Safer's End All II is a great and safe way to combat parasitic mites and insects, but there is no winning the war once something like spider mites have made it inside your garden. It is a constant battle you need to stay on top of, both with safe products like End All II and with Neem oil and insecticidal soaps too. I cannot advise you strongly enough to be careful here, my green amigos. For battles with powdery mildew I love a product called Serenade, which is a spray-on bacterium that actually consumes the mold—or at least that's how I understand it! The Serenade is pretty foul smelling though, so use within two weeks of harvest is not recommended.

"The Borg"

This is what I call spider mites (and other parasitic little bastards) that arrive in your garden via imported clones usually, but they are primo hitchhikers and can come in via peeps or animals that have just been around Borg infested gardens. I call them The Borg because they have ridden through many gardens and been attacked with a wide variety of chemicals and treatments, the whole time evolving resistances to

Serenade   End All II

> **REV'S TIP** My very best advice is, of course, to not let mites or mold come into your garden in the first place, whether they get in there through importing clones or hitching a ride when you or your friends come into your garden; hitchhiking is very common pastime for mold spores and mites. My grow rooms have been mite/bug and mold free for years, by just adhering to what I have told you above. Once you're free of these critters, the yields and quality of your plants will increase greatly, compared to the product you're used to from an infested garden.

countermeasures. This results in a "super spider mite" that is almost impossible to control without heavy work and a lot of money. This also applies to powdery mildew that arrives in your gardens via clones; it is alive, and so evolves just like the spider mites and other parasites.

Fungus Gnats

If you use any type of barnyard manure in your soil mix you may experience a fungus gnat infestation at some point. The sticky tape works great for the flying versions of these critters, but to get them in the soil mix in their larval state you should use a powdered BT (Bacillus thuringiensis) product; apply a very little bit to the top of your soil in all containers and anyplace else you store soil that is in use recycling or ready to use. All your soil needs is to be inoculated and it only takes a very small amount to accomplish this. After applying to containers, simply use a hand sprayer to spray it into the soil a tad and that's it. It will take about two weeks before you see the massive decline in the fungus gnat population, but the good news is since the BT is alive, it stays around and keeps working forever basically. I have never seen this product bother earthworms whatsoever.

Hot Shot no-pest strip

Now, once all the gnat larvae are gone, the BT seems to also leave the soil, so if in the future you see any signs of the gnats returning you can easily reapply it. Another application method I like to use is mixing up about 1/8th of a teaspoon of BT powder with about a quart (or a liter) of good water and just hitting every plant in my garden with a little bit of this water— super easy and very effective. Once again, while the gnat larvae (in

A good powdered BT product by Safer

the soil) is being handled by the BT, just hang a few of those sticky and twisty flypaper things to help knock out the flying versions.

Bio Control Method

I have used living predators for things like spider mites in the past and it didn't often work very well. The problem, as I saw it, was that the predators that eat the spider mites cannot tolerate common grow room environments, which are normally hot and dry. The predators usually need climates below 75°F and above 60% humidity. As fate would have it, however, spider mites love hot and dry conditions. Be sure to consider these factors before purchasing any predators. Outdoors (or in greenhouses that don't get too hot) these bio-predators work much better, in my experience.

Intake Vents

These will need to be screened off (if they draw air from the outside) to prevent rogue parasites from being sucked into the garden. I am still to this day a big fan of nylon stockings for this purpose. They allow airflow for passive intakes and work pretty well as a filter too.

GROW ROOM TOOLS
OF THE TRADE

A well-equipped grow room is essential to get you smoothly through a TLO grow. Here are some things I would recommend getting!

- Fire extinguisher. Please get one of these that is rated for electrical fires.
- Turkey baster (I own like 7 of them). They have a million uses.
- Cloning unit, or dedicated cloning space. Clones make life easier on a TLO medical grower. Never use clones to grow from unless they came from you; clones bring problems in to your garden like mites and mold for starters, and it gets worse.
- Sharp and clean scissors, several pairs of several sizes, including larger shears for harvesting.
- A pH meter that you KNOW is accurate. This is really important for the reliability and accuracy. If you only get one pH meter, get a good soil-testing meter. A liquid meter is always a good idea too while learning TLO, and I highly recommend Hanna brand only for liquid pH meters.
- Get a TDS meter because they are cheap. For troubleshooting and diluting certain things, these meters rule.
- Opaque tea maker/bubbler. I use a regular old one-gallon plastic pitcher for this purpose.
- Back ups for things if you can, things like bulbs, ballasts, water pumps for cloners.
- Tarps for the floors are a must for protection from spills and stains.
- Measuring spoons, Floral (tie-down) tape, and a pump sprayer are all highly recommended, and if you don't have good air movement you will want stakes handy for extra support fast.
- A high quality (quiet) venting fan. I just love Elicent fans for this job.
- Grow tents are awesome as long as they are high quality and light tight.
- A dedicated TLO tea brewing location that is fairly dark and warm is a huge plus. Teas are magic indoors because they bring in waves of diverse and nutrient-rich microlife.
- Digital timers. Get digital ones please! This makes everything so much smoother and another great reason to use 400 watt or LED lights is that it is easy to get digital timers for that wattage.

CHAPTER 3

Starting Your TLO Grow

By now, you should have a good basic set up in your grow room and understand what TLO growing is about, to some degree at least. All that's left now is to get your final equipment and start your first TLO grow!

Container Choices and Size Considerations

This is an interesting part of TLO growing, and one that seems to confuse people a lot. I will try to make this as basic as possible, because once you get this, you will agree that it's very simple. For your first TLO grow, you can start off by estimating 1 foot of growth per 1 gallon of container space. As your skills with TLO develop, your container sizes will be determined by how you like to build your soil mix/containers.

TLO can grow big plants in small containers

These are your basic black pots and they require catch trays underneath of a size that both catches enough water to allow the plant to soak it back up within 30 minutes (any excess water in these trays needs to be removed after 30 minutes) and to allow for good airflow. Select pots that have a lot of drainage holes in the bottom; this is important for any size pot. Catch trays that hold too much water or are too tight/close to the drainage holes (these are also air holes) will not work out too well. You don't want standing water in these trays for longer than 30 minutes due to anaerobic concerns with lack of air to the roots underwater. (See the self-watering style of pots next.)

> **REV'S TIP** Outdoors, in full sunshine, avoid using black or dark colored containers because they will absorb too much heat and become harmful to the soil microbial life and the roots, which will make the plant suffer. You can even paint black containers white with latex paint (on the outside only) at least a week before you put any plants in them.

REV'S TIP Try using pumice rather than perlite; you only need to cut your mix by volume by 10-15% using pumice, it retains water and nutrients, plus it is highly favored by bacteria; and cannabis does love her bacteria dominant soil. On top of all that it is much cheaper than perlite—try it you'll like it.

In the photo of the self-watering style container you will notice the very bottom of it is filled with perlite; you don't have to do this but I highly recommend it. This allows the perlite to wick up (suck up) any water leftover in the built in catch trays via capillary action. These type of pots are supreme for TLO and enhance life (aerobic microlife especially) with superior aeration. The catch tray is also designed very well so that roots at the bottom of the pot aren't forced to be underwater. The plants will detect the perlite and grow special roots down into it that can "drink" up water very quickly while being very resilient to being underwater. I call these type of roots water roots and they are very thick; the same type of roots a plant in the ground would grow if it found an underground aquifer. *Imagine that?*

These pots are a little more expensive than your average ones but well worth the investment in my experience; in fact, these have been the only pots I use for flowering plants for several years now. Under 400 watt lights I use the 11-inch version of these pots—approx. 2.5 gallons—and under 1000 watt lights I would use the 13- or 15-inch ones—approx. 3.5 and 4.5 gallons respectively. If I am flowering a longer sativa, like a 16 week flowering type, I would use the 13-inch size under a 400 watt light. I have tested all these formulas myself, several times.

Standard growing pot with appropriate catch tray

My very favorite self-watering style pots

Using these pots is a snap. Watering them using the TLO philosophy is easier because there is no need to water twice, and I sometimes water using just the lower tray, filling it up. I do this during the last 10 days of flowering exclusively and this really finishes up plants *nice!* Also I use the bottom tray and fill it up when, say, I am not sure if the pot feels

light enough for a full watering, but I'll be gone all day. That's a perfect solution right there because you know your plant will be alright and not dry out too much but you don't risk over watering her. Over watering is a very common problem for new TLO growers.

Smart Pots and other fabric style soft pots are really helpful to the living soil mix and the plant by providing *plenty* of air to the roots and to the living soil. In really warm grow rooms, or dry and hot greenhouses, or dry hot outdoors, you will need to use larger container sizes, unless you don't mind watering them at least once per day, and oftentimes I have had to water them three times per day, running flowering plants about 3

Smart Pots are
well aerated

feet tall in 3 gallon Smart Pots indoors. Just a heads up, mis amigos.

Right now, I have a pretty small personal garden. I flower under 400 watt Eye Blue lamps. Vegetative growth goes on under my LED lamps, and I also sprout under these lamps as well. I start out germinating in those little flats made for sprouting your veggies and flowers or whatnot in. Once sprouted I usually move the seedlings into 3-inch square pots

Germinating flats and keg party cups

for about two weeks, then up to 1-gallon pots for about 30 days. I then transplant into either 2- or 2.5-gallon pots to flower. My finished plants are usually about two to three feet tall, and yield two to three ounces of prime TLO bud each. These figures of course will vary greatly with different genetics. (See my additional germinating info later in this book.)

The keg party cups of the 16 ounce plastic type are, generally speaking, a bad idea as containers, and the problem is lack of good aeration. With only a couple of holes in the bottom, setting them upon flat surfaces really makes the soil mix inside hurt for air, and so too does all the life that breathes air. You can fix these by making a lot of holes in the bottom, then setting them on a grid type surface, slightly elevating the air holes for better air access. Another option is many holes low on the sides about ½ an inch above the bottom. Bottom line: If you insist on using these, make them air friendly because the microbeasties, roots and worms all love them some air.

> **REV'S TIP** Don't go too cheap with your choice of bagged soil mix or this could cause you problems down the road. In TLO growing we recycle our soil; you don't have to, but I'll show you how. Also, try to avoid soil mixes with a lot of peat moss in them. The peat moss, when recycled, tends to sometimes cause the soil mix pH to dive through the floor, and extreme corrective measures need to be taken. Finally, avoid using clear plastic cups. Both the plant roots and the microlife prefer the dark, so any light on the roots is detrimental. I like Ocean Forest and Happy Frog soils by Fox farm, and every potting soil Gardener & Bloome (G&B) makes.

Imported Clones and TLO

Think REAL hard about doing this, my green friends. I highly recommend that you start your plants from seed and then make your own clones to use from then on. Bringing in clones from friends, shops or clubs, in my experience, almost always results in some kind of nasty ass parasitic hitchhiker, like powdery mildew, spider mites, root aphids or thrips, not to mention any killer viruses or pathogenic microbial life that may be on board. Get some decent seeds; find me at Kingdom Organic Seeds (kingdomorganicseeds.com) and I will fix you up with some born and bred TLO beauties. I recommend not going with feminized seeds if you plan on doing any breeding with them, but apart from that, it's your call. Just use some good genetics and your garden will be so very much more productive and happy than if you're using inferior bottlenecked or otherwise messed-up genetics. Come on over to the forums online at *Skunk Magazine* because that place is full of great people and, as far as I know, some decent genetics. Visit the Kingdom Organic Seeds page on Facebook, James Bean Co., and Hemp Depot online to check out the only authorized distributors of KOS genetics.

Organically Grown Seeds and Seed Storage

In some of the older cannabis books from the 70s or 80s, such as *Marijuana Chemistry* by Michael Starks, you will note how they say that "wild" cannabis seeds tend to stay viable much longer than domestic varieties, and the reasons for this are a mystery. Actually, in my experience it is much simpler than that: It is the use, or non-use, of synthetically delivered nutrients that makes a huge difference in how long the seeds will stay viable for, even in perfect storage conditions. Synthetically bred seeds will last about two years on average just lying around before experiencing a huge drop in viability/germination rates. Organically bred seeds will stay 100% viable for at least five years on average under the same environmental conditions and normally for way longer.

Beautiful home bred organic seeds

To correctly store seeds, all you need to do is put them into an airtight container with no light leaking into it, and then store it in the refrigerator (or freezer). Seeds stored in this manner will stay good for at least 10 years before any loss of viability, and in the freezer I would say the period is more like 20 years. These time frames are based on organically bred cannabis seeds. It comes down really to heat, light, air, and moisture. All of these will be detrimental to seed storage. If storing seeds in the freezer, take extra care to package the seeds so they cannot move around. If they collide with each other (or the container) too hard when frozen, fractures can occur that will kill the seed. Basically, the viability period of seeds is determined by how long and how often they are exposed to temperatures above 60°F or so. I have bulk storage cannabis seeds that I like to freeze, but if I have seeds that I plan to germinate in the next five years or so I like to keep them in the refrigerator. You can freely switch between freezing and refrigerating as well, in my experience.

Pollen Collection and Storage

This is pretty straightforward, so I have just a few points to share with you regarding this. You can flower a male all by itself and just collect the pollen for later use. Containers for storage of pollen should also be both light and airtight. I prefer to use small glass bottles, which I wrap up in black electrical tape and label before putting into the refrigerator. I would not advise freezing pollen. Pollen stored refrigerated like this can be used at least six months later and will still be highly viable—but only if stored correctly!

Once the males start to flower and throw pollen (about two weeks after changing the photoperiod to 12 on/12 off) just shake a flower cluster gently over some wax paper or aluminum foil. A lot of flowers will also fall into the wax paper, and I find that running the whole lot through a regular old kitchen strainer works great because you never want anything else but pure pollen for storage, or else mold will likely destroy it all. I let the pollen sit out in the *dry* air for about a day (out of any real heat or direct light—or wind!) before using a tiny funnel to pour it into my little storage containers, and then I label and date them.

Once you remove a pollen container from the refrigerator for use, make sure to let it come to room temperatures first—about six hours—then remove however much pollen you will need quickly, and seal the remaining pollen back up and place back into the refrigerator. Repeat as needed until the pollen runs out.

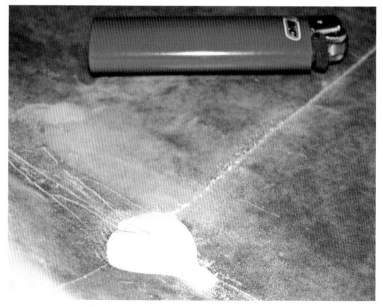

Pollen collection and preparing for storage

All Natural Germinating Road Rules

Germinating in TLO growing is just like germinating in any natural growing dynamic. Make sure there are no synthetic nutrients involved whatsoever! If you are one of those people that likes to germinate in wet paper towels, more power to you. I like to sow the seeds directly into soil mix in germinating flats. To do this, just keep them pretty shallow, and don't plant them deeper than about ½ an inch or so and all should be well. If you go with the moistened paper towel method, make sure your paper towels are not too wet, but also that they don't get too dry. I would always use something other than distilled or reverse osmosis water, due to the fact that when the little roots poke out, they can actually find uses for the small amounts of dissolved minerals in something like spring water. Bottled spring water is all good here. Germinating them in paper towels using distilled or reverse osmosis water causes their roots to find zero nutrient sources upon making their appearance in the world. This does not make for a supernaturally happy sprout, and that's how we want them from start to finish in TLO: Supernaturally happy!

Sprouts are so cute

The magic living TLO soil

It's really all about the living soil when it comes to sprouting, and if you have ever had trouble germinating anything, even avocado seeds, just try them in a living TLO soil mix and you'll see how quickly they will respond by sprouting. Something happens when those new little roots come out and they make contact with a true healthy living soil. You don't need weak soil mix for sprouts, not at all; sprout them in the same soil mix they will be growing in. The Supernatural Soil Mix Recipe 2.2 is perfect for sprouts, and so is the tumbler recycled mix. Sprouts that are germinated directly into living soil—no paper towels or glass of water—will be healthier and heartier with greater vigor, in my experience.

Nice genes Baybee

REV'S TIP For germinating seeds try: One part earthworm castings, to one part quality bagged soil mix (like G&B brand), to one part TLO soil. This is a very recent addition to the book, as I have been testing different blends for results germinating and this is the best one I found, to date. TLO soil can be a bit much for things like older (or synthetic bred) seeds; KOS seeds are all TLO all the time.

Importance of Good Genetics in TLO Growing

I don't want to redundantly beat you over the head with this, but if you have done any reading about growing cannabis, you already know how very important the role of genetics is in the happiness and health of your garden. Judge it like so: Unless you are pretty skilled with organics indoors—if you have at least a few successful grows under your belt—stick with hybrids. You will hear a lot of people throw around the sativa and indica ratio stuff, but if you ask me it all comes down to flowering time. Anything that takes 11 weeks or longer to flower is (most likely) a sativa dominant, in my opinion. Sativas can take as long as 20 weeks indoors, and until late December outdoors in the Northern Hemisphere. Anything that takes 10 weeks or less is an indica dominant variety (most likely), with pure indica varieties sometimes flowering in as little as six weeks. There are a few exceptions, as there always are in nature.

As a rule of thumb, the more indica dominant a plant is (like Hashplant/Kush) the more it will enjoy soil mix pH ranges above 6.5, and the more sativa dominant the variety is, the more it will favor soil mix pH ranges of 6.5 and below. Pure blood sativas and indicas can be a little tricky, and the longer flowering sativas when grown indoors in containers especially require fairly advanced skills. Don't worry, I will tell you all about them a little later. Don't use seeds from cannabis you bought, as these are more often than not pollinated by hermaphrodite female plants, and the seeds will also fairly often grow hermaphrodite plants that end up making seeds and ruin your sinsemilla (seedless) harvest dreams!

REV'S TIP You should grow from seed, clone all you want from that (selected) stock, and keep it around, if you choose, for a couple of years. Make some seeds with it, and then move on, starting from seeds again. If you think about the big picture, you will agree it's a no brainer. Your plants (old clones) suffer breakdown at a cellular level when you artificially prolong the life of a plant programmed to be an annual (to die and be reborn by seed every year). At about the two-year mark you will begin to note some weaknesses in resistance to disease, parasites and some loss of vigor as well. These aren't huge declines, but they're noticeable for sure if you are looking. Also, I believe older clones have particular weaknesses to viruses, as I have seen whole gardens suffer before from a mystery "plague" that killed all the older clones but left all the seedling plants standing healthy. Just some stuff to toss around in your dome.

Long flowering sativas are no sweat

Continuous flowering tent

Continuous Flowering Using the TLO Methodology

Continuous flowering means your whole growing dynamic is staggered, allowing you to place one plant, or two, or however many you want into

Continuous flowering areas are always stinky

a flowering room/tent at a time. Then about two weeks later (or however you like to stagger it) you add a few more, and so on. This way you are constantly harvesting fresh flowers approximately every two weeks.

This also allows you to run many different cannabis varieties at once all flowering for a various number of days. You can pay extra attention to trimming/drying/curing of smaller harvest numbers at once. Light distance is not an issue just using a "booster chair" that is simply a plant container turned upside down underneath any plant that needs to be closer to the lights;

A fantastic KOS sativa breeder

simply remove the "booster chair" once the plant reaches the desired height. Before you attempt this, I suggest you get really good at judging when any given plant needs watering, because you will only *very* rarely be watering all the plants at once in a continuous flowering room. This also has the advantage of not having to use as much water at once, and I like this a lot because I use two five gallon jugs in my garden, and I never have the need to use more than six or seven gallons at a time. Normally it's more like one to four gallons per watering.

Sativas and Continuous Flowering

This is an awesome flowering style for popping a long flowering sativa (or three) into your continuous flowering room/tent. Since you are always putting in and harvesting out shorter flowering varieties, you never need to experience any herbal "droughts" because your whole room/tent is full of a long flowering variety of cannabis. You can adapt this dynamic in a lot of cool ways, like 50/50 where you place half the plants that fit in your flowering space in at once, and then wait a month and add the remaining plants into flowering; this way you are essentially harvesting half as much, twice as often. Much cooler harvest times, and I hate trimming endless plants at once, ugh. The continuous flowering style allows me to harvest a couple or a few plants every two or three weeks. Each plant harvested brings two or three ounces of prime bud. I run two tents using 400 watt Eye Blue metal halide bulbs for flowering lighting as you should well know by now; in the hot summer months I often flower under LED for cooler running temps so I don't need to run a mobile A/C unit.

Recommended Seed Banks

KOS (Kingdom Organic Seeds) at: kingdomorganicseeds.com

This is my little organic seed company, and I am a decent breeder with some tasty genetics that I mix, stabilize and match. If you can find any KOS seeds, try them out. If you are looking for them look at Hemp

Depot online in the KOS section, also check out local Washington State KOS retailer jamesbean-company.com. Visit the Kingdom Organic Seeds page on Facebook and come on over to the Skunk forums online and say "high". As a rule of thumb, organically bred seeds tend to perform better in organic growing environments. If you did not get your KOS seeds from me or at the above locations, I cannot stand behind them. If you have any questions about KOS seed sources just ask me on the Kingdom Organics Seeds page on Facebook or go to kingdomorganicseeds.com directly.

Serious Seeds

These guys have been around for a long time, and I have never heard one bad thing about them. Many of my friends have grown from their seed stock and have been very happy with the results. Their seeds will cost you a bit more, but in my opinion they are worth it. Try out their White Russian (regular/normal) genetics for a serious ass kicking, and a very tough plant with large yields that's easy to grow!

Chunky Cherry Malawi from KOS grown to perfection
by TLO grower Eli173

Doctor Atomic

What a groovy character this guy is! Not only is he a nice dude, his genetics are fantastic. Thai Lights is a really great choice from the Doc's seed selection for those of you who prefer a unique and up-wardly mobile high; I loved that one myself. However, there are several great strains to choose from, so make your decision according to your grow room specs.

Hemp Depot

This source has always has been a straight shooter and I have gotten some great genetics here in the past. You can find my KOS genetics there when you stop by in the KOS section.

Sannie's Shop

Sannie has always done me right, and I just had to get some of their Blue-berry Sativa and Walhalla! Fast and secure, as well as being nice fellas.

Riot Seeds

www.riotseeds.nl

This is a seed company owned by a friend of mine for like a decade now, Matt Riot. He has some very dank varieties and he is a competent breeder, in my opinion, so check him out.

SOIL MIX ADDITIONS: QUICK REFERENCE

It is very important that you cook (pre-process) any newly blended soil mix if there are raw elements added; don't add an extra cup of kelp meal or something just before transplanting plants into it, because they will not dig it. Even things like dolomite lime need to be cooked first into the soil-mix to keep it uber friendly to the microbeasties and the plants. Below is a quick reference guide for TLO soil mix additions.

- **Soft Rock Phosphate:** Micronized (solution grade) soft rock phosphate will bring phosphorus and sulfur and will also hold the nitrogen in the soil mix and keep it from escaping into the air as a gas (ammonia).

- **Bone Meal:** Always use some of this when growing all naturally TLO style, and fishbone meal is also all good. Bone meal raises pH and adds beneficial Ca along with slowly available phosphorous and nitrogen.

- **Earthworm Castings:** You want living earthworm castings here if possible; Gardner & Bloome has bagged castings that are still very alive and healthy. Sterilized or dry castings are a distant second choice here. Earthworm castings do NOT need to be cooked before using.

- **Greensand:** A great source of slow and steady minerals and a lot of potassium (K), just as the plant wants it. Greensand will take the pH up a bit due to the high potassium levels. It also adds to soil structure in a good way.

- **Blood Meal:** Powerhouse of nitrogen (N) with a big shot of iron as well as plenty of trace minerals. This really lowers the soil mix pH and will generate actual heat if there is a lot of organic matter due to the high populations of microlife feeding and reproducing. Careful, this stuff can be as dangerous as it is wonderful!

- **Feather Meal:** This brings long-term nitrogen and calcium as well, and endures much longer than blood meal. Always nice to have some N laying around for the plant if she wants some. Only nominally effects soil mix pH.

- **Alfalfa Meal:** Alfalfa meal packs high nitrogen and great potassium (N and K) as well as an exotic growth hormone called triacontanol. Worms also love this, but you need to be careful because the high nitrogen levels can generate actual heat like blood meal can, and this heat can kill roots. Use this in moderate amounts.

- **Kelp Meal:** Full of exotic growth hormones and enzymes as well as massive trace and micro nutrient diversity. Also high in potassium (K) and great organic matter with a dash of nitrogen.

- **Perlite:** Perlite aerates a soil mix and keeps aerating it, as opposed to bark mulch, which processes too quickly. Use small nugget sized perlite if possible for the greatest aeration.
- **Coconut Fiber (coir):** Most coconut fiber is way too fat with salts. Either fully rinse your coir or get it pre-rinsed like the Botanicare product called Cocogro, which awesome for worm farms and all TLO applications. Good amounts of potassium and also takes pH up a bit; all good effects!
- **Guanos:** Never use raw bird or bat poop; this will kill your plants. It has to be composted first. Tons of powerful N, P, and micro/trace nutrients galore; awesome organic matter for microbeasty food! Chicken poop is extra kick ass if your chickens are at least semi-free-range so insects and other diversity enter their diets.
- **Rabbit Poop:** Awesome stuff. Don't confuse how this works outdoors and how it works indoors in living containers; raw, it will very likely kill your plants, so cook it first. Great levels of nitrogen so it will cook very warm too, like blood meal and alfalfa meal. Feed your rabbits über-healthy stuff and their poop will be incredible all natural fertilizer.
- **Farm Animal Manures:** Always hot compost these first. Full of great mineral salts, with good nitrogen and potassium too along with vast trace and micronutrients. Usually a little salty so use carefully. I like to keep any manure of this type low in my container (Steer Manure Layer) to start with so any excess salts go out the bottom without passing through the rest of the soil mix.
- **Oyster Shell Products:** Down to Earth makes a great powdered version of oyster shells. I use this and the crushed version; awesome calcium and trace minerals, slow and steady release, plus a great place for bacteria to anchor to and colonize. Also has positive effects on soil structure.
- **Bark Mulch:** Always, always mulch your containers! I use shredded bark for this, any bark will do, just avoid walnut or cedar.
- **Cottonseed Meal:** If for some reason your soil mix's pH is too high, then you can cook in some of this to drop the pH pretty effectively while also adding great nitrogen and trace nutrients. Awesome microbeasty food, especially fungi.
- **Rice:** I like to add a little of this anytime I mix up a new batch of soil mix for cooking, and I do it for a couple of reasons. First of all the fungi really seem to love it! Secondly, it is full of calcium and iron, two very important nutrient elements for healthy happy plants and microbeasties.

VARIOUS AERATING AMENDMENTS OVERVIEW

Vermiculite: is an extremely light (when dry) softer type of aerating amendment, spongy even. If I were using air pots (breathable fabric type containers) I would for sure have vermiculite as my number one choice (with pumice as a close second choice). Vermiculite actually swells when saturated, and then shrinks back again as it loses its moisture levels. So, this offers very effective inner aeration for containers with uber outer aeration, like those fabric type containers. Vermiculite does tend to break down into "dust" more rapidly, and since I use smaller flowering pots with larger plants in them, I actually use about a 50/50 vermiculite/perlite blend in my recycled soil mix which I use as about 20% of my total soil mix.

Vermiculite is neutral pH (7.0) and runs a high CEC value (caution exchange capacity) and can hold approx 30x the amount of water that soil can hold per equal volumes of each. Also, due to the CEC value, it also attracts many good nutrients: literally, electro-chemical magnetism. Microbeasties love porous surfaces that hold food in place for them to colonize. If you are using vermiculite as 100% of your aeration, I would recommend a 25% cut with it, in other words, three parts soil-mix, to one part vermiculite.

Okay so one of the "spooky" things about vermiculite is that some years ago it was learned there was asbestos in some vermiculite out of the Midwest (USA)—early 2000s I believe this was. Anyways, no longer a huge deal, just get vermiculite that says asbestos free. One other consideration about vermiculite is, it seems to me from what I have read, the fact that fungi really seem to like it as do bacteria.

Perlite: is super light and does not absorb any water; it is also a neutral pH value. Perlite does however, hold water along its porous surfaces, and bacteria and fungi both enjoy the presence of perlite, and this is a highly effective aerating amendment. If you are prone to grow smaller plants in larger containers, or if your environment is humid and cooler, this would work well as an amendment for you, and I would use it at about a 20% cut; in other words, four parts soil-mix, to one part perlite. Perlite takes a long time to break down, and even in very small particle sizes it still does the job, so if you recycle your soil, a lot of your perlite will roll over into your next mix, meaning you add less and less as you recycle more and more times.

I am unaware of anything particularly bad regarding perlite, but getting the horticultural type is likely a good move in my opinion. Perlite works really well in combination with clay type soils outdoors in raised beds, when combining some of the local soil with your raised bed soil-mix, and you can go very light here in this example, cutting your soil-mix by like 10% with Perlite will work fine, as Mother Nature will see to a lot of aeration herself.

Pumice: is very light when dry, pH neutral, and does indeed absorb a lot of water, but initially floats in water. Pumice is fast becoming a favorite aerating amendment of mine, as I have been testing it out for about 6 months now at the time of this writing. Pumice is about as all natural as it gets, simply put, volcanic (and highly porous, like 90% porous) rock/glass, and per my understanding, does not break down for centuries. So a big advantage when recycling is you don't ever need to bump your soil mix up with more pumice; just your earthworm castings need additional aeration amendments. Even perlite will break down into dust over several recycled uses.

Pumice has good CEC value, and is highly favored by bacteria; many kinds of fungi actually do not occupy it. Cannabis favors a bacterial dominant soil environment, so this is another cool little bonus here in my eyes. I have been using it as a 10-15% cut in some of my recycling soil mix and I like what I see a lot. I would bet I will be talking to you more about pumice in the near future. Right now I have to source mine about a two hour drive away. It seems like something that might be really astounding, and hardly anyone really is on to it, yet—let's just see about that, so stay with me my esteemed amigos, as I intend to continue my experiments with pumice.

CHAPTER 4

TLO Medium: Your Living Soil Mix

True Living Organics Growing Style

A TLO grow is a huge shift in a growing dynamic and actually turns the clock back, way back, to the style plants have been growing under in the wild for millions of years. I often refer to TLO as a "just add water" growing style, and done correctly, it certainly is that. This style relies on the strength and power of the relationship the plant has with the living soil mix. Using the same style that plants have been using themselves for millions of years, but inside of a plastic container and under high-intensity lamps may seem counterintuitive, but the basics of that all natural outdoor style are transferable to any sort of set up, and I will show you how it is done. This technique does require a little faith. The microbial life needs a little time to reach a balance, or equilibrium, in the soil mix, and while you're waiting for this to occur you need to resist the knee-jerk reaction to use liquid food. Instead, you just need to let nature work its magic. Using the higher root temps to leverage the supernatural life levels in the containers is what it's all about.

A well-used TLO supplement station

Just like when they're in the earth, your plants' roots can find various things underground in TLO containers. Creating a perfect medium is a big part of the "just add water" growing style, because you have to skillfully add various elements, not only in different ways, but in differently balanced ratios. Does that sound hard? It isn't. All you have to do is copy my recipes and pull off a harvest or two, then you'll see what I'm talking about. After that, you can dive deeper into learning why things work so well in TLO if you wish and become a TLO druid yourself. Everyone's style will evolve. The TLO philosophy highly respects what we don't know about life in the universe, as we recognize happiness in any life form via observation. It's not what you look at, it's what you see.

For ten bucks a piece, myco fungi is well worth the cost

REV'S TIP You can buy myco fungi off the shelf at higher end nurseries and grow shops, and it comes in both granular and water soluble forms. Most believe that cannabis uses only the endo subspecies of myco fungi, but I still use both endo and ecto versions and the brand Down to Earth offer several versions of these along with beneficial bacteria. You could go with something like Great White myco fungi, with beneficial bacteria as well. I recommend going with quality/freshness here if you are able.

Mycorrhizal Fungi (myco fungi) is an incredibly important addition to any all natural growing style that uses containers. I used to use this in a granular form, which I would apply just before any transplant, and I set the root ball right on top of some of the granular myco fungi. Additionally, I have a soluble form of the myco fungi as well (Great White) that I apply with *chlorine-free* water, about a day after sprouts emerge, or right after I put newly rooted clones in the soil the first time.

The myco fungi cannot live very long without living plant roots to attach to once moisture is added to the store-bought products containing them. This is why you must always bring myco fungi in yourself, in my experience. It is of utmost importance in TLO growing, and without it, your plants will have smaller yields, not be as pretty or vigorous, yada yada. You can get all the bacteria and other kinds of beneficial microbial life into your soil mix by using fresh, healthy earthworm castings or high-quality compost. If the earthworm castings still have living worms in them, then they are extra awesome and full of microbial life. You don't need to keep adding myco fungi to the same container or to the same plant; you only need to do it once. Myco fungi are alive, and so this is an inoculation, and the myco fungi will reproduce and evolve like all the other life in the containers.

Please note that myco fungi can be rendered useless very quickly if you use chlorinated water, synthetic nutrients or any raw liquid nutrients on your containers, especially those with higher levels of available phosphorus in them. TLO living teas and pure water should be the only liquids you ever pour on your TLO living soil.

Bagged Soil Mixes

Gardner & Bloome (G&B) Blue Ribbon Blend Premium Potting Soil, with mycorrhizal fungi added, is a great and inexpensive soil mix to use, as is their regular potting soil. I also like to cut my mulch on top with G&B Harvest Supreme mix, as it contains chicken guano all composted as a great all-purpose nutrient source—this mulch cut can attract fungus gnats so be ready just in case it does. Something like Fox Farm's Ocean Forest is also an old favorite of mine, though it has just gotten rather expensive lately, and you can get an equal amount of soil mix and comparable quality for half the price with the Gardner & Bloome soil. Now, using TLO methods we are pretty much going to become sustainable growers after a

Great organic soil

The rewards of TLO growing are supernaturally elegant

harvest or two. However, for things like freshly rooted clones, or for some quick soil if you forgot to make some, it's good to have some bagged mix lying around, and these are a couple of good ones (not the Harvest Supreme for freshly rooted clones). Essentially any good quality organic soil mix will work. We make our TLO soil mix *supernatural*, with about 25% of it being a good bagged organic mix like these.

You can use just straight high-quality bagged soil mix to grow in, you will just need to use larger (quite a bit larger) container sizes is all, and you will also have to add some perlite to help with aeration. However, don't expect results anything like you will get using the TLO soil mixes I give you in this book. See later in this book for simpler TLO solutions.

TLO Soil Mixes

Okay *mis amigos,* here's where the really good shit starts to happen, and right off the bat I am going to tell you that you don't need to be paying $20+ per bag of soil mix—really! You certainly can if you want to, and that is almost always good organic soil mix in my experience, but you don't have to spend a lot to get a great soil mix. My favorite, which is pretty much available all over the USA at the time of writing, is by Gardner & Bloome (G&B now), and you can get it for about half the price of other bagged soil mixes. I get mine locally for about $10 per 2 cubic feet bag—which is nice! This stuff is every bit as good as anything out there commercially available, and all it needs to supercharge it for TLO growing is the addition of some perlite. I would cut this soil mix by about 20% with small nugget-sized perlite, and I would also add about 1 cup of greensand per cubic foot of soil mix before using it on cannabis. Just make sure, above all else, that your soil mix is ALL or 100% natural and/or organic, without any synthetically chelated nutrients present.

I use bagged soil very rarely these days, but to start out with the three-pronged methodology of TLO you will want to start with a high-quality bagged soil mix. What I do use bagged soil for is planting freshly rooted (aero-rooted) clones, and for this purpose I use the Gardner & Bloome Blue Ribbon Potting Soil (comes with some myco fungi added already but I still give them a shot of Great White). See my freshly rooted clone mix to follow.

Normal TLO soil that you amend and cook for growing in will be much too strong and powerful for freshly rooted clones and will kill them quickly. The clone mix is very important, and so the Blue Ribbon brand (G&B) with added mycorrhizal fungus (myco fungi) is what I use here for my bagged soil. For starting TLO mixes the Supernatural Soil Mix Recipe 2.2 way, I use the plain G&B Potting Soil. Also, for your first soil mix (Supernatural Soil Mix Recipe 2.2 further on) out of the gate, using the three-pronged approach, you will want to use a bagged soil mix of quality, and for this first mix you don't need any myco fungi because this soil will need to "cook" for 15-30 days prior to usage; myco fungi don't live that long without living roots to join forces with. "Cooking" is an imperative step that you must become savvy with, and undercooked soil mixes will really grow sad plants. Always cook soil well.

REV'S TIP ALL soil mixes and soil elements, including mineral elements, need to be cooked BEFORE living roots arrive on the scene. Even Dolomite lime needs to be cooked first, so when you are getting your soil mix or your containers all put together, don't be tossing in extra bat guano, or Dolomite lime, or even kelp meal (mixed globally with your soil) because if it is not cooked in yet it will cause problems. Spikes and layers are never applied where living roots are present either. My motto for TLO growing is this: Always cook everything first.

REV'S TIP You will hear me referring to "the rhizosphere" in this book many times along the way. See the illustrated image of the rhizosphere to better wrap your head around what and where it is.

Cooking Your Soil Mix

First I want to help you to understand that "cooking" your soil mix is simply another way of saying "composting" or "fast composting" your soil mix. Another way to say it would be fast decomposing. This is a very important aspect of custom soil mixes, and without doing this, more times than not you will fry your plants. If you are making your own custom mixes, adding things like kelp meal and guanos that have not already been composted, and you are not "cooking" your soil mix, then this will be the cause of your problems.

It's worth saying that again: Raw, natural additives like lime, meals, guanos and manures all need to be processed in the cooking procedure before roots will be super happy in the custom soil mix. All you need to do is mix together your soil mix, get it all nice and moist *but not wet* and keep turning it over every few days for two to four weeks, or longer if you like. Ambient temperatures during this cooking process should be at least 60° F and the cooler it is, the longer it will take to complete the cooking process. In my cold garage it takes about 30 days for mine to cook. Don't worry; even over time the nutrients don't evaporate from your soil mix, so if it ends up being a year before you use it, that's okay too. Even if it seems super dry to you, the soil can still have mucho life in the micro world, using particles of water so small the roots can't even access them directly—Hydroscopic Moisture levels—and even if it does get bone dry, a large percentage of microlife can go dormant to reemerge when water comes back into the soil—the powers of Mother Nature to come back!

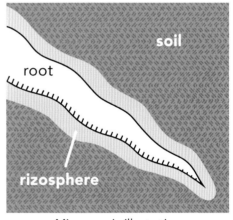

Microscopic illustration of the rhizosphere

Put simply, what cooking the soil does is allow massive amounts of microbial life to colonize the soil mix and work its (decomposing) magic on it, just like they would do in a compost pile. What else do composting

With my recipes your soil will be so healthy
even the worms will love it

and soil cooking have in common? High levels of nitrogen (N) are really effective when cooking your soil mix, just like in composting. This is where things like alfalfa and blood meal really kick it up a notch, and your soil mix will sometimes actually heat up a little while cooking. This is absolutely normal when some elements that are higher in N, like blood meal, guanos, manure and alfalfa, are added. Things like feather meal are good too, but the N release of feather meal is a lot slower than that of the alfalfa and the blood meal. Feather meal is also longer lasting and has a good dose of calcium too, which is always nice. You could also use guanos and manures effectively here as a catalyst to cooking, as these supply high amounts of available N. The only downside to manure usage indoors (even cooked) is that fungus gnats really love manure and can become a problem, so I like to use a little manure in my cooking soil mixes because it has a serious positive effect. I share a very effective fungus gnat counter measure in this book, which worked extremely well for me recently—and it's a bio-predator, so it just keeps on working.

The bottom line, folks, is that you MUST cook your custom soil mixes, period. Failure to do this will always result in disappointment, so really make sure you take this seriously. Try to understand what each element brings to the table in a custom soil mix, and right after I give you my latest and greatest mixes I will go over all additions, and why they are there, in order to help you to better understand the processes at work. Substituting things in the mix is usually a bad idea unless you actually know what you are doing, so try hard to stick to the recipe for your first few grows, so you can use a proven successful soil mix as your benchmark before you start modifying it.

Here we go my very green friends, the first prong of the whole three-pronged TLO shebang! We start out with our initial soil mix, an upgrade from the 2.1 soil mix in the original version of this book. It's more basic and less complex. This soil mix will take you into the whole recycling process if you like—seriously a good idea. Try to stay right with me, exactly, for your first run so you get that all important benchmark of wicked good success. Do your best.

You can freely dial these ratios up or down to make however much you need for your operation with some quick multiplication. Make small moves if adjusting for the power of the mix. I change things in ½ cubic foot (three gallons US DRY) measures, and I judge for at least two months.

Only for use with pure water sources, like reverse osmosis, rain or distilled water. Do not use well, tap or spring water with this recipe unless your PPM is below 20 and has healthy balanced calcium and magnesium levels.

TLO SUPERNATURAL SOIL MIX RECIPE 2.2

Let me first say that this mix was designed to be cooked first, and to be used with pure water sources like reverse osmosis, distilled or rainwater only! Also this mix is designed to be used in concert with teas, layers and spikes. You will make your initial TLO grow using this very potent soil mix. If possible, make double the amount you will be needing for a single entire grow (one run), so you can always have some recycling (cooking) while using the soil mix that's ready to go.

You don't have to be very accurate with the following four additions, just close to 4 gallons of each, and basically even ratios of each. FYI 18 gallons of soil mix = 3 cubic feet (US DRY). This recipe makes 16 gallons.

Base Mix
- 6 gal (1 cu. Ft.) organic soil mix (use a quality soil mix)
- 2 gal thoroughly rinsed coconut coir fiber (use 8 total gallons bagged soil-mix if no rinsed coir available)
- 4 gal perlite (small nugget size) OR 50/50 vermiculite and perlite—highly recommended
- 4 gal earthworm castings or quality compost (living earthworm castings, and/or living compost works best)

SOIL MIX 2.2 AMENDMENTS

- ½ cup Grow or Bloom 'Pure' by Organicare Dry (or 1 cup 5-5-5 or quality All Purpose)
- ½ cup greensand
- ½ cup ground oyster shells (1.5 cups of crushed oyster if ground not available)
- ¾ cup crushed oyster shells (1/4 cup ground shell if crushed oyster not available)
- 1 cup powdered Dolomite lime (2 cups prilled if no powdered available)
- 1 cups prilled (pelletized) fast-acting Dolomite lime (extra 1/3rd cup powdered if no prilled available)
- ½ cup blood meal
- ½ cup high N bird/bat guano (like 9-3-1 N-P-K)
- 2 cups feather meal
- 2 cups bone meal
- ¼ cup powdered soft rock phosphate (3/4 cup rock phosphate granular if powdered not available)
- ½ cup gypsum powdered (1 cup granular if powdered not available)
- 3 cups kelp meal
- 2 cups alfalfa meal (up to 6 cups if you like)
- ½ cup Azomite granular (3 heaping tablespoons if powdered Azomite is used)
- ¼ cup Humic Acid Ore granular (like from Down to Earth brand) (optional but highly recommended)
- 1 cup (heaping) organic rice (optional)
- 2 – 6 cups of steer manure or barnyard manure (optional but at least 2 cups is highly recommended)"

This mix should be moistened (do not get it soaking/mud wet!) with chlorine (chloramine)-free water, and turned over every few days for at least 20 days before use. This is what I call "cooking" your soil, and letting it get pretty dry before use is fine. The nutrients don't evaporate or anything, so no worries there. If this soil mix turns out to be too hot (powerful) for some reason, just cut it with more good bagged organic soil until you get the strength demanded by your environment and genetics. I do NOT RECOMMEND this soil mix for placing freshly rooted aero clones into, however it is beautiful for seedlings. This soil works best under higher intensity conditions, using HID (or powerful LED) lights for

---

"Cooking" your amended soil for recycling for longer than 30 days is not a problem at all, and if you can plan ahead enough, cooking it for 60 days is really just extra primo! Just make sure it stays moist.

flowering, keeping plant tops in the mid 80s (F) during lights on.

I find cooking my soil-mixes for about 20-30 days works the best for me, but I have often used it sooner, like at two weeks, and just remember the warmer it is outside, the faster the cooking processes will happen. You can use a pH meter (soil pH meter) to tell when it is done cooking too. I wait until it is between 6.2 and 6.8, which normally takes about two weeks, because as it kicks off cooking the pH will often be very low; around 4.9 isn't uncommon when it first starts to cook—perfect for blueberries, not for cannabis.

This soil mix is meant to be used along with the spike and layer TLO dynamic, and while it is quite capable of standing alone, it works *supernaturally* when you add the spike and layering dynamics. If this

Sup'r Green chicken poop is my favorite for recycling

is too overwhelming of a formula, just use the fast soil mix recipe in this book in the simpler TLO section. Your soil will yield below par results for TLO growing standards, but it will turn out some dynamite cannabis and give you a taste of what you may have been missing.

Base Mix Examined Closer

Good quality bagged soil will work fine here, no worries. You don't need to use the Blue Ribbon version because all the myco fungi will just go to waste during the cooking process. You can use the G&B Potting Soil (regular, without myco) or Ocean Forest by Fox Farm, and their Happy Frog line of soil seems to work well for these purposes. I also want to add that if you are going to be recycling your soil mix, make sure to avoid using a bagged soil mix with a large amount of peat moss in it. Peat moss tends to really favor the fungus and will cause recycled soil mixes to drop to a very low pH; I just want to make sure this stays in your head because it will kick your ass sometime down the line.

Gardner & Bloome
Blue Ribbon Blend soil

Cocogro is my favorite coconut
coir product and is great at
buffering the pH of your soil mix

Coconut (Coir) fiber is an awesome TLO custom soil mix amendment for a couple of reasons, including the fact that it seems to be a great at buffering the pH of your blend. It keeps the pH from diving too low, which is a common problem when your soil mix contains a lot of raw organic matter that has not been decomposed quite well enough. Also, as this coir breaks down, which it does fairly quickly in TLO like in any other organic matter, it releases available potassium (K) which is always an important thing for flowering cannabis. Cannabis loves her K, and the microbial life really likes the coir fiber as well. Unfortunately, this means that coco coir isn't a great amendment specifically for aerating your soil mix; always use perlite (or a 50/50 perlite/vermiculite blend) for superior TLO soil mix aeration. Another thing to note about the coir is that it is also a able to hold a lot of water for its size, and this is always a big plus when you favor growing and flowering in smaller container sizes.

Coir also is really good for the soil structure, especially as it relates to the CEC values of the soil mix. Last, but by no means least, always get coir that has been thoroughly rinsed with fresh water. It will say so on the product, and keep in mind that sea salt is all natural, but those salts are detrimental in a TLO soil mix in any great amounts. Organicare has a fantastic coconut coir product called CocoGro that has been left outside for a season or two and thoroughly rain rinsed. Be aware that coir products can fly all natural/organic labels, including OMRI rating labels, but still have way too much salt for TLO growing. You could just get brick coir like the stuff from Down to Earth, then expand it and thoroughly rinse it out (flush it) yourself; normal tap water is fine for doing this. I use the CocoGro for the convenience and quality.

Rule of Thumb for Using Coir Fiber Ratios

Basically you want to cut any soil mix with *some* of this stuff (pre cooking) by 10% or so (at least) in my experience, per total volume of the soil mix—not counting my specific recipes for the Supernatural 2.2 and Recycling mixes. You could even go 5% if monies are tight, or availability is lacking. It really brings good things, so just try to add some if you can't get much.

Perlite is the stuff, boys and girls! Aeration in your living soil mix is über-important, and you can pretty much cut any bagged soil mix with perlite by at least 20% to accommodate super natural levels of microlife. I recommend smaller nugget-sized perlite, and this is straight-up good math. Smaller particles equal more surface area, and more surface area equals more aeration. Perlite is not consumed by the microbeasties for food so it hangs around for a long time, which is why it works so well. Shredded bark and coconut coir are both examples of organic stuff that sucks to use for aeration in TLO growing, due to the fact those both decompose *rapidly* in a TLO soil mix.

Another less well-known property of perlite that any TLO grower has to love is its very porous and pH-neutral nature, which makes it a beautiful place for microlife to colonize. Think of it as lots of miniature versions of artificial reefs out at sea that coral builds upon; in your soil mix the microlife does the same thing, attaching to the perlite for essentially the same reasons.

Note: I highly recommend using a 50/50 vermiculite/perlite ratio to replace pure perlite amounts stated in this book; you could use 100% of either vermiculite or perlite really, however, pure vermiculite will hold a LOT of water and be a bit less efficient at the aeration than having perlite present—just a little FYI.

Earthworm castings and compost are both superior additions for several reasons and it's important to have one of these, if not both, for a top-quality grow. Bagged versions of earthworm castings can be good or poor, and a good rule of thumb for TLO growing is this: If the earthworm castings still have living worms in them, they are primo! This is the prime reason you are using earthworm castings or fresh compost: To bring in microbial life, including micro-predators like

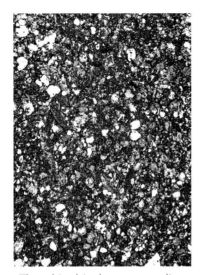

The white bits here are perlite, an essential part of any living soil mix

These bagged earthworm castings are of a high quality and great for TLO use

amoebas and other protozoa, along with beneficial nematodes. These guys are every bit as important as the bacteria and fungi in your soil mix! Avoid anything that is sterile, or has been sterilized, and use your nose; nothing should smell bad, but should have a very clean and earthy aroma. You will get to know that smell if you don't know it already. It is easy to learn how to compost, and there is a ton of info at your local library or on the internet.

Another great benefit of using either or both of these amendments is that they contain vast amounts of organic matter all broken down into humus. Humus translates into fantastic nutrients for your plants that are very available.

Dry Amendments Examined Closer

Grow "Pure" by Organicare (or All Purpose 5-5-5) is an all-purpose, dry all natural nutrient. Any good one will work, but it is important that all three of the numbers be around the same. Several brands of all-purpose dry nutrients will have numbers like 4-6-2 regarding N-P-K values, for example. The potassium (K) is an important nutrient for cannabis, so always opt for more equal numbers if possible. I particularly like the Organicare all-purpose Grow (and Bloom) granular "Pure" nutrients with 6% added calcium. Additional calcium is almost always a plus in cannabis growing, especially when using a living soil mix, because the microbeasties love their calcium almost as much as the plant does.

Greensand is very important indeed, so do not underestimate its super powers! This element enhances soil structure and airflow through the soil mix, and also supplies potassium and over 30 trace and micronutrients/elements in a very slow-release form. Potassium (K) and Iron (Fe) are two of these. Greensand is not something you would use to counter a deficiency so much as you would use it proactively to back up supplies of things like iron and potassium to *avoid* a deficiency. If you recycle your soil mix you'll really get the most bang for your buck here because greensand keeps giving for years. Back in the olden days we used to use manure and greensand at the bottom of the holes we dug to plant our outdoor cannabis. For many years we treated this combo like a big secret because it really made that much of a difference, so be sure not to leave out the greensand in your soil. Tomatoes, strawberries and cannabis all love this amendment. I have noticed greensand tends to work well with barnyard manures, just don't overdo it.

Oyster shell products are uniquely capable of a few excellent contributions to a living soil mix. Cannabis loves calcium, and microbial life needs and loves calcium as well. Oyster shell products provide slow-release calcium and other nutrient elements, and that's the first benefit,

Left to right – ground and crushed oyster shell

Prilled and powdered dolomite lime

but wait, there's more. When building soil mixes you always want to be somewhat aware of the ratio of calcium to magnesium, which should be around 5:1, in my experience, and heavier on the Ca is alright too. Oyster shell products essentially provide a pure calcium carbonate which breaks down very slowly, releasing calcium for the microbial life, and hence the plants, to use.

If your magnesium levels get too high, like from too much molasses, bad things start to happen, and so this can be a tricky dance, due to the fact that cannabis also loves a lot of magnesium. Dolomite lime (see below) brings in magnesium along with calcium, and I use this in my mix as well.

I use two grades of oyster shell products, the ground and crushed versions. The crushed is just larger pieces than the ground, which has a course, sandy consistency, and the main difference here is the length and the strength of the buffering effects the calcium carbonate has on the soil mix. This is another benefit of using these shells. I like using the ground shells as a buffer for spike and layer mixes that use things like guanos and blood meal in them. If not for the buffering effects of the ground oyster shell, those products would really take the pH down very low for a longer time. In addition, calcium is one of the most underrated nutrients ever in cannabis growing, because cannabis loves slowly released calcium, and I even use crushed oyster shells in my worm farm food (kitchen scraps and leftover cannabis matter with shredded junk mail) to make sure my castings are calcium rich. I advise you to keep calcium on your mind when customizing soil mixes and you will be one happy camper!

You can see that I use plenty of the crushed shells globally in the Supernatural Soil Mix Recipe 2.2 and this is because I like the larger pieces for their artificial reef qualities aiding bacterial colonization, and for the length of time it takes them to break down. Elements in a living TLO mix tend to break down much faster than is stated in many organic grow books. My crushed shells last about 90 days (max) from what I can see. I have read a lot about how oyster farms really seem to help out the environment and it all seems pretty sound to me. Make sure to source some oyster shell products and not to omit them as they are a very special addition that likely enhances the soil in many more ways than I or anyone else knows. The results speak for themselves, so go that extra mile if ya got to.

Dolomite lime is *really important* for you to understand, especially when growing in containers. It is made from both calcium and magnesium, and cannabis plants love plenty of both of these elements. There are many kinds of lime, so be careful here. Using hydrated lime, for example, could very easily become a disaster in a living soil mix. Dolomite lime is what you want here, and I use this as one of my major magnesium sources, with the others being CaMg+ liquid by General Organics and molasses in my TLO teas. There are several grades of Dolomite lime, so let's take a look at these first.

There is a granular version of Dolomite lime that looks like tiny reddish volcanic rocks. This is a very dense form of Dolomite, and really takes a long time to break down. This grade is virtually useless in container growing in my experience, in the short term for buffering purposes. There is also a granular version that looks like small shards of rock salt,

---

REV'S TIP Dolomite lime (or garden lime as it's also called) is the only lime to use in TLO growing. Avoid any others. Dolomite lime buffers the soil mix rather than just raising the pH like any other lime will do. Dolomite lime likes to take pH up, but no higher than 7.0 as a rule of thumb, and if something tries to take your soil higher than 7.0 the Dolomite lime will take it back down; nice, right? A soil mix pH of 7.0 is all fine in TLO growing, and so are 6.2 or 7.5 even! It all depends on what genetics you grow, and how well evolved your microbeasties are.

and this works well for global applications for buffering. It is also a quickly available source of calcium and magnesium for all the life in the container, including the plant! Another granular type is called "prilled" or "pelletized" and this looks like little round reddish or brownish balls with a soluble shell of Dolomite lime, with a smaller harder rock in the center normally (but sometimes no hard center)— sort of like a Peanut M&M. This stuff is awesome for global applications. Both the prilled and the rock salt-looking granular types say "fast-acting" on the bag, and this is a key phrase to look for when shopping. fast-acting granular Dolomite works really well, but I would avoid the granular dense rocks that are not fast-acting. Powdered Dolomite is an essential element in a custom soil mix and it is also *super important* to "cook" (as above) any soil mix to which you have added Dolomite lime to, globally, or root damage is likely to happen.

Dolomite lime is one of my major sources of magnesium and calcium, and it also buffers the soil mix pH from dropping too low (and from climbing too high.) The powdered version really helps to keep bacteria happy during the soil mix cooking process, because they tend to not like any big drops in the pH of the soil and the microbeasties we want far prefer pH up in the mid 6 to high 7 range. Fungi can take over the container soil mix if the pH drops super low in my experience, and once they have a certain level of dominance they seem to me to kill most or all of the bacteria present. Plant roots are not happy in the super low pH ranges that these fungi enjoy, and these fungi also tend to keep the pH down as well from their natural exudes.

When mixing a lot of powerful nitrogen sources like blood meal and bird/bat guanos with Dolomite lime, make sure to see the section below regarding soft rock phosphate, to avoid losing some nitrogen from your soil and other bennies.

> **REV'S TIP** High-phosphorus bird and bat guanos are very acidic and will quickly lower the pH of your soil mix, so it is not a good idea to mix these globally I think. This is due to their highly available levels of phosphorus, which are proven to discourage fungi and algae in things like golf course ponds and home water features. This includes the all powerful and beloved mycorrhizal fungus, so I recommend not using high P bird and bat guano as global soil additions. You'll notice the 2.2 soil mix calls for zero high-phosphorus bird or bat guano mixed globally, and there's a good reason. However, I do love high-phosphorus guanos for top dressing and for spikes for flowering plants, and the slow P release of things like bone meal.

All natural additives like guanos need to be cooked after adding them to your soil mixes, just like everything else

Blood meal is a great soil addition but one that needs to be used with care

Blood meal, bird and bat guanos are powerful nutrient sources, and the N-P-K ratios are usually about 15-0-0 for blood meal and 12-8-2 for bird and bat guano. These are essential additions for a super natural living soil mix. Blood meal can be as dangerous to use as it is powerful, so have great respect for the amount of damage this can cause if you overuse it. Guanos are only slightly less dangerous for all the same reasons as blood meal. These elements both catalyze large populations of microbial life, and you will need to make sure that any soil mix that contains these is well cooked, due to the rapid decomposition that happens while the microbial life has these high power sources of nitrogen and organic matter to feed off. This reaction is the same one that happens in compost piles when high nitrogen is added; even additions like grass clippings, manure or alfalfa have enough nitrogen to really get things cooking big in a compost pile, and all the decomposing will happen very fast with true heat from all the motion of the microbeasties feeding and colonizing.

As far as levels go, even ½ a tablespoon of blood meal in a gallon of soil mix can overdose cannabis plants if it is not cooked first (unless top dressing where this rule can be bent). The same approximate measurement applies to guanos, as they are only slightly more forgiving. I like to use these elements in layers as well as spikes. You will read in books about blood meal lasting six months in a soil mix, and in a TLO living mix it *might* last two months, but only for one month of that will it give massive nitrogen release, in my experience. Organic matter tends to decompose very quickly in a TLO environment, and bat and bird guanos only really rock the nitrogen for about three weeks and last about four or five weeks total. There are, of course, plenty of slow-release nutrients that will continue to be released through the natural cycles of the microbial life, but the "big bang" effects of those nutrients burn out rather quickly. However, they do deliver some serious results while highly available.

For vegging older clones I like to top dress them about once every 10 days with a little bat guano (9-3-1 for N-P-K values), You will notice the P value is ⅓ of the N value. I find this is a good rule of thumb for the ratio of P to N for these vegging plants so you don't encourage them to flower (or try to flower) under vegging photoperiods. Make sure the total P value is under 5 as well. In a standard 5- to 7-inch pot I would use about ½ a teaspoon right on top, in a couple of smaller piles out by the pot edges; always keep any top dressing away from the base of the main stem!

Feather meal is very out of the ordinary to some folks, and it is a fantastic element in your TLO soil mix. N-P-K ratios on this one usually are around 12-0-0, but it is a very "slow burning" source of nitrogen, and it lasts for a long time, even in supernatural living soil mixes. Calcium is another benefit from feather meal, and while reading this book you will hear a lot about how very important both nitrogen and calcium are to all the soil life. Take a look at any good, all-purpose, dry organic fertilizer and you will see "feather meal" in the "derived from" portion of the label. There's a very good reason for this; this slow-release nitrogen is wonderful for larger flowering plants in an all natural garden.

I use the Down to Earth brand feather meal

You might read various opinions regarding feather meal, such as someone's belief that the bio-availability of the nitrogen in feather meal may be very low, or how nematodes and bacteria are the primary decomposers of feather meal. I can tell you firsthand that it is an extended-release nitrogen source, and just like any other nutrient element you can certainly overdose your soil mix with it, causing problems for your plants. Feather meal is a byproduct of the poultry industry, and another perk of using it is that it brings calcium to your mix. Feather meal gives a continuous medium to slow nitrogen feed for about 10 weeks or so in my experience, and I dearly love this stuff. Hoof or horn meal or healthy fur/hair are all good substitutes for feather meal.

Bone meal is a big deal and what it brings to the table in your TLO mix is giant yields during flowering plain and simple. In the previous version of this book I did not recommend steamed bone meal for using globally with my mixes. However, that has changed and I have been using steamed bone meal for about five years now with great success. You can use steamed or unsteamed bone meal. It's all good, mis amigos.

Bone meal brings in a fantastic "slow burning" form of P, along with calcium and N. The plants love this stuff and they have been used to using it for millions of years. These days I use a custom mix of about 50/50 regular bone meal and fishbone meal, but either one works fine by itself as well.

Whitney Farms Bone Meal is fine to use, as is Down to Earth brand bone meal

Fishbone meal is awesome all by itself too. The high P numbers are like the high P numbers in your average bone meal, and the P is locked up and bonded with calcium just like in bone meal. I use a 50/50 blend of each because I always welcome good diversity in my source matter for elements, both products are easy for me to get, and I just know in my head—or feel that I know—that fish bones are special and bring some extra goodies to the table beyond their N-P-K values.

Soft rock phosphate and rock phosphate are important short- and long-term ingredients. I like granular rock phosphate (RP) for a super long-term phosphorus source. I recycle my soil mix, so I am really playing into the strengths of long-term nutrients like this. Soft rock phosphate (SRP) is powdered, and along with delivering very available phosphorus at a medium to slow release

Fish Bone Meal by Down to Earth

rate, it also has many other trace, micro and secondary nutrients as well. This addition also has a really big benefit for any custom soil mix, and that is how it seems to counter a natural chemical reaction in the soil mix. When high-power nitrogen sources (like blood meal, alfalfa meal and guanos) meet lime, some of the nitrogen is "lost" because it will often convert into ammonia (gas), which is just another form of nitrogen. (*Don't* use ammonia on your plants!) However, when some powdered SRP is added to your custom soil mix, the ammonia in gas form (A.K.A.

This granular rock phosphate has N-P-K ratios of 0-3-0

This powdered rock phosphate is a little lower in phosphorus

nitrogen loss) does not occur. If you have ever mixed up a batch of soil and let it sit, then noticed it smelled like ammonia, this is why. I keep the ratios of SRP in the soil mix on the low side, due to the fact that too much of it (or any readily available phosphorus) will inhibit the good fungi, including the mycorrhizal fungus as well as causing other issues. The SRP and RP both also put beneficial CEC properties into your soil mix, making things like the available calcium "sticky" in your soil so it will stay and not be flushed away during watering.

Gypsum is one of the most underappreciated elements in many all natural gardens, and what it brings to the table is all good for cannabis especially. Some ancient organic growers from around The Pygmy Forest in Northern California used to rave all the time about gypsum, and how the slow-release sulfur enhanced natural smells and flavors in the final cannabis buds. Gypsum is calcium and sulfur (calcium sulfate), and many people believe, as I used to, that it radically lowers soil pH. The truth is, in my experience, that it will have this effect in soils that are already very low, and I think this is due to the fact that fungi really love gypsum. Outdoors gypsum works wonders on big clay-packed soils, even just used on top, and aerates them by somehow bringing in fungus to thrive on the clay minerals, I believe.

In well-buffered soil mixes gypsum is a fantastic addition with a bunch of slow-release calcium and sulfur. Sulfur is very dangerous to add straight in its elemental form, due to the fact that sulfur will plummet your soil pH quickly and completely! Also, straight elemental sulfur additions can attract certain bacteria that we don't want in large populations in our containers' soil mix. Bringing in some sulfur via the gypsum is awesome because of the slow-release availability. As long as your soil mix is well buffered, gypsum will not radically drop the pH value of your soil mix, but instead will only slightly lower it without any problems. In container growing especially, you really need this addition both for the calcium and sulfur—but mostly for the sulfur. It's a really safe and great way to bring the sulfur into the mix, so don't omit it! You can use this either powdered or

I use powdered gypsum and love it for its slow-release sulfur

granular, and if you only have access to the granular version, just double the ratios stated; triple the ratios if the granular size is larger. A very common first mistake that peeps make with their first recycled soil is a lack of enough sulfur. This looks a lot like an iron deficiency, with yellowing up top and stunted growth. Using gypsum correctly will eliminate this issue before it ever starts.

Kelp meal is always a great addition that brings in some fantastic elements and raw organic matter. It's rated high for nutrient values and other beneficial aspects, such as around 60 minerals or elements, 12 vitamins and 21 amino acids. I like it a lot in any soil mix, but it really needs to be cooked first, because as it breaks down it can tend to take the soil's pH down pretty hard.

You can easily go overboard with liquid seaweed and kelp products—as well as the soluble dry versions. This is a rookie mistake, and one that many of us have had to experience to know of its importance! Take my advice and be very careful not to overuse the liquid or soluble dry kelp and seaweed products. It is pretty tough to overuse dry kelp meal (not an extract), but anything is possible. Kelp and seaweed concentrate products are also very full of available potassium (K), which is always a good thing in moderation. Always read the labels on any products before you use them.

Down to Earth's kelp meal needs to be cooked before it is used, or it can drag the pH of your soil mix right down

Alfalfa pellets, once composted, bring loads of
lovely nitrogen to your soil mix

Alfalfa meal or pellets are awesome sources of nitrogen, and alfalfa
is super bio friendly due to its beautiful carbon to nitrogen ratio, although this results in rapid decomposition (cooking) that you don't
really want happening with living roots on the scene. Rapid decomposition is a great thing, you just don't want it happening around living
roots is all; that's why these things need to be composted or cooked
first before living roots have access to them.

Make sure if you use the *pellets* of alfalfa that they are clean of any
kind of additives. Alfalfa brings many trace and micronutrients to the
table, as well as an exotic, all natural growth enhancer called *Triacantanol*
that may also help fight off parasitic fungi. I feed this stuff to my worms,
top dress with it and use it in spikes and teas almost always. Alfalfa is
one of the cornerstone elements of TLO soil mix going *super* natural.

REV'S TIP Alfalfa meal is great to add to worm food or to a
soil mix before it is cooked. I prefer using the pellets
of alfalfa, but you need to check these out thoroughly to make sure there
are no additives in them and that they haven't been "enhanced" with any
vitamins or minerals if sold mostly as barnyard animal feed.

Azomite has over 60 mineral and trace elements and this is really one
of my big power hitters as far as long-term mineral nutrients—especially micronutrients—are concerned. It is available in finely powdered
or granular versions. I use the granular version in my soil mix and the
powdered version in teas (very minute amounts) and sometimes lightly
in spikes. Azomite powder is finely ground, and if you can get hold of
it, I *strongly* recommend its usage.

Humic acid ore is very interesting, and I use the granular version made by Down to Earth. This is really a catalyst that aids in the availability of micronutrients, phosphorus and potassium. It also acts like a wetting agent, allowing water to penetrate and permeate the soil mix extremely efficiently. This makes for excellent soil structure and enhances soil tilth as well. This also seems to lower the pH of the soil mix slightly, but if it is used at my suggested ratios this will not be a problem. Find this product or one very much like it—you won't be sorry.

Rice is a cool thing to add and I use Basmati rice. I always noticed my fungi stayed happier and kept my phosphorus and calcium levels more available to my plants when rice was in the

Down to Earth's humic acid ore

soil mix. I always use it and I never forget or omit it, as I feel it is a very important component in a TLO soil mix—and it's cheap! Optional for sure, but try it!

TLO Soil Mix for Freshly Rooted Clones

You should always use a very mellow soil mix when planting freshly rooted clones. I have found that freshly rooted clones need a mellower soil mix than sprouts do. It is a common mistake to put freshly rooted clones into a soil mix that is too heavy with dry nutrients or to feed them with liquid nutrients too soon. Both of these actions will very often end up frying the plants. Here is my tried and true soil mix for this exact application:

TLO SOIL MIX FOR FRESHLY ROOTED CLONES

- 2 part Gardner & Bloome Blue Ribbon Potting Soil (or comparable all natural soil)
- 1 part earthworm castings/or quality compost
- 1 part perlite (smaller nugget size is better)—a 50/50 vermiculite/perlite mix is also recommended.

Try to always avoid touching new roots to bone-dry soil mixes, and don't forget to inoculate with some mycorrhizal fungus and get that plant's relationship with the beneficial fungus up and running.

How To Plant Your Freshly Rooted Aero/Bubbler Clones Into Soil

Using the mix above, I like to place the freshly rooted clones into small three-inch pots for about seven to 10 days, before transplanting up to seven-inch pots. No layering or anything is done to the three-inch pots, *and mellow is the key here*; just the soil mix above and nothing else. Here's the step by step:

Step One

Make sure the cloning soil mix is moist—not soaking wet—just before using. Just use your finger to make the hole in the soil as shown in the photo.

Step one: make hole not quite to bottom of 3-Inch pot

Step two: plenty of healthy roots to plant with

Step three: swirl or spin roots down into hole gently

Step four: don't forget to mulch

Freshly rooted and planted TLO clones

Step Two

In the photo you can see about my minimum root growth required, in order for the clone to survive a transplant virtually 100% of the time. More roots are even better, and less (or no) hardening off will be needed with more clone root mass.

Step Three

You can actually spin the clone slowly between your fingers while lowering it gently into the hole. Don't push hard as this can break off roots. Gently scoot soil from the sides of the container towards the clone and *gently* compress soil immediately surrounding the clone. Remember to water the first time using a myco fungi soluble powder or add granular myco to the soil mix *just before* filling the three-inch containers with that batch of clone soil.

Step Four

After watering add your mulch layer on top, and although pure shredded bark is fine, I actually use a mixture of 2 parts shredded bark to 1 part coconut coir fiber here. Keep plants a little farther from intense light sources for a couple days if they need hardened off.

Balancing Your Soil Mix and Your Water Source

It is super important to keep the quality of your water on your mind all through your growing period. If you are not using a pure water source for some reason, and you think your water is low enough in dissolved minerals to be able to use, then I'll trust your judgment. Just make sure to use carbon filters if it is city tap water, because chloramine will devastate a living soil mix. Generally water up above about 100 PPM should be filtered; however, there are exceptions. Don't gamble here if you have any doubts, please.

Say for example you want to use your city water; you have the carbon filtering all figured out, and your water registers about 60 PPM on a TDS meter. Since most of the dissolved minerals in any city tap or spring/well water will be calcium and magnesium, you just have to compensate for this by perhaps tweaking the Dolomite lime ratios in your TLO soil mix. Your calcium and magnesium ratios are very important, and you need to have considerably more calcium than magnesium at all times. If you are using spring, well or city tap water and you are having problems it could very well revolve around these ratios of elements dissolved within that water; it is not uncommon for well water or city water to be pretty high in magnesium, iron and sulfur to name a few. Too much magnesium in your living soil mix and the whole soil structure seems to break down; the soil takes on a real "crusty" state and becomes choked of good air flow (aeration), which is of course über-important for a living soil mix to have. Plants tend to die slow and horribly when magnesium levels are too high.

Powdered (or Micronized) Calcium Carbonate

I want to say that this element (available easily online) can be used in very small amounts added directly to your water before use to correct for certain genetics that require high pH ranges (like Kush and Hashplant types and many of their hybrids). This is also effective at combating a screw up that is a common mistake, killing off a large number of your soil bacteria by adding something "bad" to your teas, like something high in organic acids. The fungi are resilient to pH drops and with that help from you they can dominate the containers' soil mix .See more about this in the troubleshooting section.

COSMOPOLITAN SPIKE TIPS FROM THE REV

Spikes are especially good at bringing in things that you don't want added globally in high ratios to your soil mix. Especially things like phosphorous (P) and sulfur (S) and silicone (Si) to name a few. Just remember the main important thing in any spike is to have a decent amount/ratio of something that decomposes fast and that microlife love to colonize. So along with things like soft rock phosphate, bone meal, and high P bat/bird guano, you can add some smaller amounts of things as needed, like gypsum (sulfur and calcium), or diatomaceous earth (DE) with calcium (Ca) and silicone (Si); both Si and S, as well as P can be needed when using recycled soil, for over the top quality and potency, in my opinion. Things like smells and flavors become much more pronounced.

You can make your spikes complex or more basic, it's up to you, just broadband your nutrients as I said, and use something like alfalfa meal along with kelp meal as about ¼ to ⅓ of your total spike recipe/volume. This initiates a lot of microbeasty activity around the spikes' outer layer and allows the spikes to be permeated by air as the green additions decompose and are used for food, and transformed slowly (from the outside in) into beautiful plant food.

Another great rule of thumb for any spike is make sure and have a high power N source also mixed into your spikes. Having experimented with a lot of blends, I find that overall for my big N source for all spikes I use blood meal for veg spikes, and fish meal for my flowering spikes. Blood meal is like 15-0-0 and dried fish meal is about 15-10-2 for their N-P-K values.

CHAPTER 5

Spikes and Layers

Spikes, Layers and Zones, Oh My!

Here's the first real big twist that separates TLO growing from most other all natural styles. Spikes give a lot of power to hungry cannabis indeed. The TLO soil mix in this book requires additional elements in the container to achieve supernatural results, and spikes are essential for bringing in more important elements in "bulk" such as nitrogen and phosphorus, to name two biggies. Nitrogen and phosphorus cannot be added globally to the soil mix in sufficient amounts using smaller container sizes, or there would be big problems with the microlife, and that is never a good thing in TLO growing. Using spikes will give the smaller container sizes much greater punch, especially during flowering. The plant roots can access the concentrated N spikes for their immediate N needs, leaving more of the global N for

To create a hole for spiking, use something like this: my 2 gallon container spiking tool

The spike should go almost to the bottom of the container

Place the tool all the way in, as deep as you can

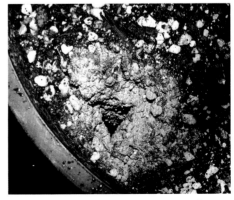

Now fill up the hole with your spiking mix and watch your plants thrive!

the microbial life to use to reach supernatural colonization and metabolism levels. "It's a good thing," as Martha Stewart says.

Remember to NEVER make spikes where there are living roots present! I rarely use any spikes during vegetative growth these days, and the only time I spike is when transplanting the plants into their flowering containers. Here are a couple of the main spike mixes I use, made from all natural dry elements blended together:

ALL PURPOSE HIGH N SPIKE

- 1 part blood meal
- 1 part bone meal
- 1 part high N bat/bird guano (N-P-K example 9-3-1)
- 1 part feather meal
- 1 part kelp meal

FLOWERING SPIKE

- 1 part feather meal
- 1 part high P bat/bird guano (N-P-K examples 0-5-0 or 2-10-1)
- 1 part bone meal
- 1 part kelp meal/alfalfa meal (50/50 blend)

In the picture of the store-bought Jobe spikes, you can see the concept that we're going for. You push these spikes into the soil mix for your roots to find and feed from. In TLO you can use these spikes if you like, as long as they are all natural, or you can blend your own—like I do—with the recipes above. Just make holes in your containers' soil mix and fill in those holes with the spike blends. I find a wooden dowel about ½ an inch wide makes for a great spike hole maker. You want to make the spikes BEFORE there are roots present, so I always do this during a transplant, then the roots can find the spiked nutrients and adapt to them accordingly, once those nutrients have already started decomposing (cooking).

Using these spikes, along with the layering techniques that I will explain later, allows you to add additional amounts of powerful all natural dry nutrients without frying your plants, which is what would likely happen if you mixed these nutrients in much higher ratios globally into a soil mix. Dry nutrients like bone meal and blood meal can be used in spikes very effectively. My spikes are placed close to the container's outer rim, so the roots have to grow a bit to reach them. In a

This TLO grower uses a
hollow tube for spiking

Note the uniform holes
and easy application

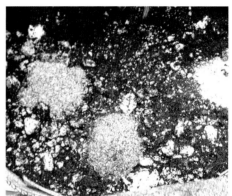

Spikes visible in the TLO pot

Spiking is vital to a TLO garden

typical two-gallon container, planning for a nine to 10 week flowering plant with a final height of about two to three feet tall, I would have my spike hole about ½ an inch wide and about ¾ the height of the container (soil height in container). So, if my container was one foot tall, let's say, my spike holes would be about nine inches deep. A surprising amount of spike blend can be poured into these holes. After filling the holes, simply add a small soil topper and give the spot a gentle pack down with your finger, and then add the shredded bark mulch layer on top. Water everything fairly well.

Do try your own blends too, but please use the ones suggested first, as these are proven winners in TLO and will help you to understand the fundamentals before you embark on trying your own mixes. Please don't assume you know what you are doing and become careless. TLO philosophy requires a decent amount of un-learning. Basically, we have all been "taught" to grow by the nutrient companies

TLO spikes ready for use with handy labels

(corporations) favoring their bottom line. You simply don't need their liquid fertilizers; just use real all natural/organic matter.

Remember this: Spikes work best when they are on the thinner side and I never make spikes with a larger diameter than about ½ inch. Outdoors you can break this rule no worries, just make sure there are no cannabis plant roots present at the spike locations! The anticipated drip-line is where to place your outdoor spikes. Also, always use two or four spikes per plant when transplanting into the flowering containers, because you always want half the spikes to be flowering type and half to be higher N type.

In the case of layers, you start with the "floor" of the container, which is just the bottom (inside) of a growing container before any soil mix has been added. I normally apply a thin splattering of a custom high-nitrogen blend here on the floor, along with some all-purpose dry nutrients, before I

Commercially available organic spikes

HIGH-NITROGEN TOP/BOTTOM LAYERING BLEND

- 2 parts blood meal
- 1 part kelp meal (or kelp/alfalfa meal 50/50 – recommended)
- 1 part feather meal
- 2 parts high-nitrogen bird or bat guano
- 1 part ground oyster shells (a.k.a. "oyster shell flour") or bone meal

add any soil mix to the container. I put another thin layer of just high nitrogen blend under the bark mulch layer on top of the container mix once filled and spiked.

Note: I no longer use any kind of middle layer, as it just seemed to me to be more hassle than it was worth. You can kick ass using just the bottom and the top along with spikes and BOOM! However, there's nothing wrong with using the old style TLO middle layering if you like it and it works well for you.

I believe that it's better to use layers and top dressing with higher nitrogen blends. Remember that the microbeasties need a lot of N for themselves, in order to build their biomass (bodies) as well as more N needed to attend to the plant's needs. Top dressing with more bal-

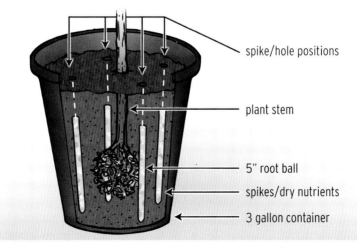

Here you can see the perfect position for
spikes in a container full of soil mix

I use ground oyster shells by Down To Earth. A quick search on Amazon online will show you a lot of options. If you get your oyster shells crushed, like from a local oyster farm, just give them a good rinsing off before use to remove any excess sea salts. Oyster shells are an important component in TLO growing. They are a pH balancing/buffering element (they raise the pH somewhat) as well as a slow-release calcium source, a bacterial catalyst and an aerating amendment—nice!

Here is a custom TLO layering blend that's high in nitrogen

anced guanos, something like a 10-8-2, is all good for flowering until about week four. At this point all available N additions should cease or be nominal. Later into flowering you can top dress with things like high-phosphorus bird or bat guano, but I would do this in a couple of smaller piles right on top of the bark mulch layer and away from the base of the main stem, then simply spray it in a little bit with a pump sprayer using good water. This way you don't expose a large area of the surface of the container mix to the effects of the high P guano, and specific microbeasties can colonize the guano quickly when it's localized. This is exactly what I do for my flowering plants about three or four weeks into flowering. About two or three teaspoons of high-P guano per two to three gallon container is all you need. I let at least 10 days go by (usually 10-14) before I top dress with high P guanos again, if ever. When using the high-P types of guano, a little bit *really* goes a long way.

> **REV'S TIP** Get good at troubleshooting and you will be a happy grower. Powdered soft rock phosphate is an awesome addition to your spike recipes if you need additional P; especially if your soil pH is above 7.0 which will cause the P (phosphorus) from bone meal to be harder for the plant to get and use.

When I build any container for transplanting into, I always use a little bit of this high-N blend on the "floor" of the container and just under the bark mulch layer. These are two highly aerated areas of the soil in your containers, and the microbial life will really get their groove on without having to rob any N from the plant in the short term.

Earthworm Castings and Fresh Compost are two of the most effective organic matter sources you can use in all natural cannabis growing. The upsides are many, and the downsides are few. None, in fact; you just need a little space. It is important for you to understand that when growing the TLO style, we do not like the word "sterile"—except, perhaps, in regard to our cloners. You always want fresh (living) castings or compost if possible; fresh and healthy. The smell should be earthy and clean, not stinky (outhouse like) at all. It is relatively easy to find bagged earthworm castings, and if there are living worms in the bag of castings, everything is beautiful! Any beneficial life that fresh (living) castings or compost brings to your soil mix is arguably its greatest benefit. My favorite brand of bagged earthworm castings is called Worm-Gro by Gardner & Bloome; I'm not compensated in any way to say that, I just happen to be a big fan. Talk to your local nursery or grow shop and see if they will order them for you if they do not carry them already. These are wonderful castings, totally full of life and nutrients that your plants will love. TLO is all about life, and living compost or earthworm castings not only bring in a wide array of bacteria and fungi species that are super beneficial, but also micro-predators like protozoa, and good

I can't recommend perlite strongly enough; no indoor living soil mix is complete without it

The TLO growing methodology causes severe dankness

My personal earthworm farm—indoors

guy nematodes, which are essential to a supernatural soil food web of life, just like lions and hawks are needed in nature—for the all important balancing effect they bring.

As a rule of thumb, the larger your container size is, relative to your plant size, the mellower you can be when building your containers. I use spikes full of dry nutrients like blood and bone meal because I tend to flower in smaller (two-gallon) containers, under 400 watt Eye Blue Halide lamps. However, if I were doing the same size finishing plants in three-gallon containers I could omit either the spikes or the teas; I have grown out plenty of awesome plants to harvest using JUST GOOD WATER when I used large sized containers, and under 400 watt

Tray of drying cannabis matter for worms

HID lights needed 3.5 gallon sizes to truly be a just-add-water garden, using just layers and spikes.

I like to store my additional earthworm castings separate from my recycled, ready to rock TLO soil so I can keep the tote full of worm castings—and plenty of living worms—a little bit moister. I'll mix them together about a day before I am going to transplant. To do this I simply mix up however much soil I think I will need for the job. On a large scale this would be a pain in the ass, so mixing them at a ratio of about 3 parts soil to 1 part castings or compost works well. FYI worm castings are considered already cooked for TLO purposes. Always leave containers holding living soil mix or castings/compost open, at least a little, and never seal them up!

Make no mistake about it; access to good quality living worm castings or compost, or having a home worm farm/composting system that is healthy, is actually the second prong of the TLO methodology, with the Supernatural Soil Mix Recipe 2.2 being the first prong. Let me say that the home worm farm is an awesome way to go here, and I use both a home worm farm and compost tumblers, but, bare minimum, you need to be able to cook soil and compost some organic matter—*like roots*—at the same time everything else is cooking. I'll explain all this later on in this book when I show you all the convenient and effective wonders of the compost tumblers for just these purposes! Let me tell you all about the worm farm I have first, and the latest revisions.

Having your own earthworm farm is the best option for some people, including me, and I used to keep mine actually inside my indoor TLO cannabis garden, as you can see in the picture. These days though, I have moved my worm farm out to my shed; you could use a tent outside if you wanted to, environment permitting. Once you get the hang of taking care of one of these it is super easy and beneficial in lots of ways. I even got a juicer and started eating way healthier, just so I could have a good source of worm food. They like juicer leftovers, banana peels, any veggies that have gone bad, used coffee (or tea) grounds and filters, as well as any vegetable leftovers including all leftover cannabis plant matter like leaves and stems. You should let any fresh plant matter dry out before adding it to the worm farm, and chop up the stems a bit as well; however, I don't always obey this rule and if my worm farm is running on the dry side I will add very fresh extra cannabis plant matter. Buffering the pH of all the organic matter with crushed up eggshells (you would need a LOT of eggshells all by themselves), crushed or ground oyster shells and *rinsed* coconut coir fiber is recommended. I also feed them all my paper junk mail after it goes through the shredder.

The liquid that collects from a spigot on my worm farm is very powerful stuff, and I usually freeze mine into ice cubes for using later. Warning: This can be messy at first until you get savvy. *Do not dilute the worm juice/leachate* with water before freezing. My worm juice is very high in PPM/TDS and this is likely due to the fact that I routinely add a little greensand, Azomite and ground oyster shells to my worm food; these all help to buffer the pH, as well. The excellent minerals in the greensand are quickly broken down and accessed, due to all the *living* organic activity in the proximity. This is my theory at any rate, because I know that supernatural levels of microbial life tend to require surprisingly high amounts of calcium and nitrogen. The microlife will actually steal this from the plant roots if supply is limited.

We will discuss earthworm castings and compost teas later in this book. The liquid that collects from these kinds of worm farms (which comes out of a spigot at the base) is actually called leachate or leachate worm tea/juice, but it should not be confused with an organic TLO tea. I have also found it beneficial to aerate all my worm food with small nugget sized perlite, and I leave the spigot at the bottom of my worm farm open, with a small catch tray underneath. This encourages more airflow, and it is always good to be extra concerned with airflow when you are spawning huge (supernatural) populations of microlife—*amen*. In your TLO containers, if air is hard to find, the

Frozen worm juice cubes

living soil mix can and will take air from the roots and this is never a good thing. Always be thinking of how to supply better aeration to any living medium, be it your earthworm food/castings or your containers full of living TLO soil mix.

The quality of your worm castings or compost is a huge facet of the TLO methodology. Making your own castings gets you the highest quality ones, and I will show you all some stellar additions to add along with your worm food, and how to start your worm farm for the first time. Worm farms like mine can endure some harsh environments. Last year we had a hard freeze for about five days, and even though I didn't see any worms for a few weeks after, all the worm food was still processing, and within about 30 days I started seeing worms abounding again. In higher temps, you need to be highly concerned with their need for more food (higher temps = higher metabolisms just like your plants), moisture and aeration levels, and any direct sunshine is a no-no! Having access to oyster shells is invaluable here, and they are a primo buffer with great calcium.

BOTTOM LINE: You must have access to compost or castings; the higher quality the better. You don't have to have a worm farm or composting system yourself, but you will need access to either or both of these for the second prong of TLO growing. Remember this little factoid: Composting doesn't need to be stinky AT ALL. Only if it goes

Worm farm showing worms in top tray

anaerobic will it get stinky, so once again, aeration is the key. Keep everything turned over often and aerated well, and there'll be no stinky effects! Bugs, however will love composting materials, but once it is all done composting (cooking) the bug numbers will be nominal usually. These are good bugs. Try and lose the knee-jerk reaction that bugs or germs are automatically bad and need to be killed immediately—that has been taught to you courtesy of those who manufacture the killing products you will "need." Ya follow?

Rodale's Ultimate Encyclopedia of Organic Gardening is a great companion book to have when TLO growing. This book will teach you a lot about composting properly and has tons of other great info too. It isn't cannabis related at all, and it goes into depth about numerous other plants you may want to grow. It has detailed sections

REV'S TIP You can find these farms online easily; just search "earthworm composting." It will cost you around $100 (USD) to get all set up with one like mine, complete with some Red Wiggler worms, which arrive about two weeks after the farm gets to you.

on predators and environmental needs, so check it out. I use mine at least once a month and learn something new almost every time I open it up. Once you discover the true power of all natural growing, you may well turn into a gardening dork. I did! I grow tomatoes, strawberries, herbs/spices, potatoes, peppers, corn and more using all natural philosophy outdoors in the ground or in containers and all my produce is out of this world. Grow your own all natural tomatoes or whatever and you will be in for a very pleasant surprise when you see how veggies are supposed to taste.

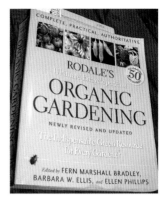

Great book for composting advice

Layers, Top Dressing and Spikes Revealed In Depth

Spikes are basically just custom dry blends for filling up spiked/poked holes in the container mix, or in the ground around outdoor plants. Outdoors in the ground, you will want to place the spikes out at "the drip line" and always well away from the main stem. This is done during a transplant so that the microlife has time to colonize the nutrient-rich spikes before the roots arrive, making the discovery for the roots much

EARTHWORM FARM TRAY AMENDMENTS

These additions are per tray of your worm farm and you mix them in with all the worm food before adding it to the tray and placing it on top of the worm farm for the worms.

- 2 tablespoon kelp meal
- 2 tablespoon alfalfa meal
- 1 tablespoon greensand
- 1 tablespoon granular Azomite
- 4 tablespoons ground oyster shell (use 1 cup if crushed oyster is used)
- 1 tablespoon granular rock phosphate (optional)
- 1 quart perlite (or perlite/vermiculite blend 50/50 is highly recommended)
- 1–2 quarts (rinsed) coconut coir

more plant friendly. Again, don't do this once a plant has put roots throughout the container, as you can easily kill your plant like this. Spikes can go top to bottom (the full container height) in length/depth, or they can be shallower; I normally go about ¾ of the way to the bottom of the containers with my spike holes. It's totally up to you and your needs. In a typical one-gallon container for vegetative stage plants, I would use two high-N spikes placed out by the container rim as usual, but only for plants I wanted to stay happier for a much longer period of time in smaller containers. These days I rarely spike my vegging plants and almost exclusively I only use spikes in flowering containers.

When you are using spikes whilst transplanting your plants into their containers they will be flowering in, it is very important you use an equal number of high-N spikes *and* flowering spikes. If you use four spikes total (recommended) always use two of each type flowering and high-N spikes.

Avoid using lime (of any kind) in spikes. I have consistently experienced bad results when adding Dolomite lime to spikes. I prefer to use ground oyster shell and things such as bone meal to balance the pH of my spikes to some degree, keeping them from experiencing a severe drop in pH from things like guanos, blood meal, and any raw organic matter like kelp or alfalfa meal. More than a couple of die hard TLO growers have told me Dolomite lime works well in buffering their spikes; so experiment if you like, but just try it on one plant first to see what you see.

Layers take on three basic meanings in TLO growing. I use two main locations for adding some extra nutritional kickers in dry form: The floor and the top—just under the bark mulch layer. The bark mulch layer is another kind of layer; it is very important and should always be present.

Spike hole filled in a two gallon container

Layers and spikes are perfect for smaller TLO containers

In the previous version of this book I had recommended a steer manure lower layer for containers. That is no longer as applicable indoors, as it can spawn huge numbers of fungus gnats—if the pots were out-doors, no worries. That steer manure bottom layer could work well; just make it 2 parts steer manure (composted), 1 part coir fiber and 1 part perlite. I also like to add a little bit of greensand to this steer manure blend, like a tablespoon per gallon of this mix.

Bark Mulch Layer Options

I like Douglas fir bark, shredded, as my baseline mulch layer; however, you could use shredded tree leaves or shredded cannabis stems or all of those together. This mulch (top) layer should be *the law* in all con-tainers. It catalyzes huge populations of microbial life up top and it does the same outdoors in the ground. This in turn feeds the plant with a rich dose of things like potassium and nitrogen along with a plethora of other available nutrient elements, should the plant want them.

The Harvest Supreme by Gardner & Bloome essentially brings in diversified shredded barks and organic matter and such, along with some composted chicken guano (normally chicken poop runs about 2-2-2 for N-P-K values). It's a little kicker for the plant about to start flowering, with great value for both P and K along with N. Also let me say that if you are doing things right in your (warm) grow room, green-house, etc., your mulch layer will disintegrate (decompose) in 30-45 days—no worries, just replenish as needed. Feel free to even go with a straight up shredded bark out of a bag with nothing else added; the power of the mulch layer equals far more than the some of its parts.

VEGGING AND FLOWERING TLO MULCH SUGGESTIONS

- 4 parts shredded bark, leaves, stems, etc.
- 1 part (rinsed) coconut coir fiber

The recipe above is a very simple and very effective combo, and for my flowering plants I make it just a little different:

- 2 parts Harvest Supreme (topsoil bagged from G&B)
- 2 parts shredded Douglas fir bark
- 1 part coconut coir fiber

Dry Nutrient Layering/Dressing Options

This section includes top dressing variations, top (just under mulch layer) layering and bottom (floor of container) layering. It is always very important to keep raw powerful organic nutrient elements, like we use in the suggestions that follow, away from the base of the main stem. It's also very important not to ever have living roots come into contact with raw organic dry nutrients until they have had a chance to cook/compost. Spikes cook from the outside inward, so it only takes the microbeasties a couple of days in warmer temps to colonize the "skin" of any spike, rendering it a rich food source for the roots—like a treasure chest! We catalyze the processing of the nutrients with some good N; remember mis amigos, the microguys need nitrogen in order to literally build their bodies, and we want many billions of bodies, so always consider the N needs of any dry nutrient layering, and especially when used as a top layer dressing.

REV'S TIP   When selecting commercially available bagged mulch like shredded tree bark, make sure it is just the bark and it hasn't been painted for esthetic value or treated in any way to make it last longer outdoors.

> **REV'S TIP** For a typical two- or three-gallon growing container, I would use about a tablespoon of any top dressing at a time, and I would space your top dressings out at least 10-14 days apart. Now I top dress with a wide variety of things, depending what I have on hand and what I feel the plant will want access to. Thinking about 10 days into the future is a good TLO practice always, and there is a two-week rhythm between what you do and when the plant most noticeably benefits from it.

Top Dressing

You can be very basic about this one, and if well done on a schedule, and not *overdone*, you can use this methodology of top dressing to replace the need for any living organic teas (I will show you about teas later in this book) and produce yields and quality near or at the genetic potential of the plants. When top dressing—immediately afterwards—I always hit them with a little water from a plant sprayer just to get it all wet and start it off processing, ASAP. Up on top with all the air it processes quickly; just let gravity and watering do the rest—slow down your bad selves.

For vegging plants, things like alfalfa meal, kelp meal and feather meal are all awesome as standalone top dressings and they work well combined in equal parts. Remember to put these right on top of the mulch layer; just make sure to not cover most of the surface area with any top dressing. High-N guano, bird or bat, is all good here in little piles, and for vegging plants, you want the P value to be a third of the N value, or less, AND you don't want your total P value to be over 5. This will keep older clones from trying to flower even under a vegging photoperiod sometimes.

For flowering plants during the first half of their flowering cycle, you can top dress with a few piles of bat or bird guano with pretty even N to P values, like a 10-8-2 or something there about. Just make sure the P is at least half the value of the N. I am also a big fan of kelp meal here as well, because of the rich K and everything else that it brings to the table to help balance the nutrients. Blending this with the guano is awesome; I would use 2 parts guano to 1 part kelp meal as a primo top dressing blend here for coming into this stage of maturity. You could blend feather meal in the mix as well at this stage, and make it 2 parts guano, 1 part kelp meal and 1 part feather meal.

For later flowering plants I use the high P bird or bat guano, and my favorite is by Fox Farm. It is a 0-5-0 for N-P-K values. I also like the

Top dressing done well pays off big

Down to Earth brand Seabird Guano with a 0-10-0 N-P-K value. Apply just like above, and feel free to blend this with kelp meal at a ratio of equal parts. The small amount of N in the kelp meal will not supply the plant with enough available N to trigger it back into vegging. A dose of available N late in flowering is a major screw up, and hits your resin production/potency negatively.

Top and Bottom Dry Nutrient Layering Variations

The blends I suggest for top and bottom layering can be spread all around the surface or the floor of the container—just keep it more like a dusting of the top not an actual layer of pure nutrients, and keep it all away from main stem. But when using a single organic nutrient, like guanos, or bone meal, I like to use them in little stripes or piles right on top of the mulch. This is especially important with bird and bat guano, and even more so with the high-phosphorus versions of these guano products. The blends that follow are pretty buffered, and whenever using things like blood meal for a layer (love the stuff) you will want a buffer in there to keep a little handle on the pH once the blood meal starts processing and to supply additional aeration and organic matter like kelp meal and ground oyster shell bring.

When I say the top layer here with these dry nutrient elements I am talking about the layer on top of the container's soil mix, just below the mulch layer, so any top layering is done just before adding the mulch. When replacing your mulch layer as you will want to do every 30-45 days or so as it processes (cooks) away, you can always add a new top layer at these times also—except after the halfway through flowering mark. When I say bottom layer, I am referring to a layer on the floor of the container, which is added *first* before any soil is placed into the container.

Organicare Pure Dry
Granular Bloom Formula

The very easiest and convenient way to accomplish these layer demands is using a high-quality all natural dry fertilizer blend, and I prefer granular for these types of fertilizers. My favorite fertilizer in this form is called Pure (Grow or Bloom formulas), by Organicare. In a typical two- or three-gallon container I would use about one tablespoon on the floor and one tablespoon on top under the mulch. If it is a vegging container, use the Grow Formula, and if it is a flowering container, use the Bloom Formula. Boom! These can stand alone as your layers if you want to keep it super simple and *very* effective as well. You always want some nitrogen in these blends to catalyze the microbeasties into supernatural status. There are some custom blends I use for these layers, and I use them *along with* the Organicare dry fertilizers. Here are some good ones.

BASIC BLEND HIGH NITROGEN

- 2 parts blood meal
- 2 parts kelp meal
- 1 part ground oyster shell or bone meal
- 1 part feather meal
- 1 part high-N bird or bat guano (9-3-1 as an N-P-K value example)

This one is a heavy hitter with a ton of power and meant to be used lightly on the floor and/or top layers of the container. Great for vegging plants, and fine for plants going into flowering on top; however, when transplanting into flowering containers I use the high-N blend only on the top layer and use the following formula for the bottom layer.

MY FAVORITE FLOOR LAYERING BLEND FOR FLOWERING

- 4 parts bone meal
- 2 parts kelp meal
- 1 part fishmeal (this will be your available fast nitrogen bump for the microbeasties down low)
- 1 part high-P bird or bat guano (like 0-5-0 or 0-10-0 N-P-K values)
- 1 parts feather meal (slow release N for plant to build big flowers with)

Now fish meal is something we haven't talked about yet. My brand (Seagate) runs at 11-5-1 for N-P-K. For a vegging plant you would optimally want your P to N ratios with less P; however, for flowering, all those fish bones bring a really potent P and calcium shot for the plant and the microlife to take advantage of. I love this stuff for just this kind of thing, and I love layering the floor of the flowering container with it. You could sub out something like bird/bat guano here in place of the fish meal as well. Just keep in mind that you will be missing that calcium using guano.

MY FAVORITE HIGH NITROGEN LAYERING BLEND

- 4 parts blood meal
- 2 parts feather meal
- 1 part bird or bat guano (high N type like 9-3-1 N-P-K)
- 2 parts ground oyster shell (or oyster shell flour)—you could sub bone meal here if you cannot source the oyster products

You could get very basic with the basic high-N blend, like 2 parts blood, 1 part kelp, and 1 part bone. You can of course experiment—just wait until you have a greater understanding of what elements bring what nutrients to the table, and how quickly and for how long. This blend really catalyzes the microlife and is well balanced. A proven winner.

You could sub out the balanced guano with fish meal here. When

BASIC BLEND FLOWERING

- 2 parts bone meal
- 2 parts kelp meal
- 1 part balanced bird/bat guano (12-8-2 as an N-P-K value example)
- 1 high P bird/bat guano (0-10-0 as an N-P-K value example)

layering the floor of a typical 2.5-gallon container for a plant that will be into flowering within a week or so, I would use about 1 tablespoon of Organicare's dry Pure Bloom granular, and about 2 teaspoons of one of the flowering layering formulas, and about 4 little piles of bone meal (1/2 teaspoon for each pile); before I added any soil to that container.

Even if I were just and only using the two Organicare Pure dry granular fertilizer versions for my total top and floor layering, I would still use the Pure Bloom on the floor (about 1 tablespoon per 2.5-gallon container) and the same amount of the Pure Grow as my top layer when going into that flowering container. The plants will need some N into flowering, so don't worry, you don't need to get too crazy with your P and I never use two high-N layers in a container (bottom and top layers) unless it is a vegging only container. I never use two flowering layer formulas in the same container, always a high N on top and the flowering layer on the floor for flowering containers.

Recycling Your Used Soil and Roots

Recycling your soil and cannabis matter (as well as kitchen scraps and more) is the third and final prong of the TLO methodology. In this method, we take the used soil and matter and give it a new lease of life by adding back in what the first grow will have taken out. The amendments discussed above all play a huge part in this, and once you start recycling your soil, you won't look back. My TLO soil mix is always recycled these days. Recycling is such a huge deal in TLO that I'm giving it its own chapter. Head over to Chapter 10 for more information on recycling amendments and my Recycling Soil Mix Recipe. It's all there, baybee!

Summary of the Three-Pronged Methodology of TLO Growing

FIRST PRONG:
Make Your Supernatural Soil Mix Recipe 2.2

Building and cooking this soil mix out of available bagged soil and some all natural amendments is your starting point. Once you make this you won't have to do it again, unless you need more supernatural soil again using quality bagged soil mix as a base, because you will be recycling this soil after you have used it. You don't *have* to recycle your soil, and if you really want to, you can just keep making Supernatural Soil Mix Recipe 2.2 to grow in; however, that's an awful waste of money and a waste of some magically delicious soil. You will likely want to make a second batch of Supernatural Soil Mix Recipe 2.2 about 30 days before you harvest your crop. This way you will always have TLO soil that is ready while some is recycling as well. I store all my ready soil in large totes that I never seal up all the way, to keep the air flowing.

SECOND PRONG:
Make or Source Worm Castings or Compost (Living and Healthy)

This is seriously a must have or a must get. Worm castings or compost are a cornerstone of your living soil, keeping it full of organic matter rich with nutrient value for the plants, and having your own worm farm is really magic in this regard because running it the way I show you in this book gives you the *supernatural* castings! If home composting, you could get a smaller version of my compost tumbler. You can compost a lot of things you don't naturally think about, and it doesn't have to be a super messy or smelly bug fest either. Try it and you might like it; again, having control of what organic matter goes into composting will control the quality of that compost. Turn it often and/or aerate it well and it won't get stinky.

THIRD PRONG:
Recycle Used Soil, Roots and Extra Plant Matter

My TLO recycled soil is about six or seven years old at the time of writing, and I buy a bag of soil about once every couple years—seriously—just for transplanting freshly rooted clones into. Try hard to get a compost tumbler for this job (and for cooking your Supernatural Soil Mix Recipe 2.2 in as well) as it keeps everything much more simple, and you could easily put one of these on an apartment balcony. After you recycle your soil the first time and grow in it again, you will see the true power of TLO!

AWESOME TLO TWEAKS THAT GO THE EXTRA MILE

Here are some of the higher end tweaks I use, and as you get more comfy with TLO you will have your own favorite tweaks as well. Just remember not to do a whole bunch of new stuff all at once because if something goes south you will have too many variables to figure it out.

- Get a little earthworm farm, or make one, and start recycling your soil, roots, etc.
- Use high-grade organic molasses for teas during flowering stages.
- Use a pure water source like reverse osmosis, rain or distilled.
- Use dry soluble kelp/seaweed products rather than liquid because they will stay good forever.
- If you use an aero or bubble cloner, after your cuttings have been in it for about 4 days, add about 10 drops of CaMg+ by General Organics and the roots will BOOM!
- Use a high end and fresh source for any microbial life (like Myco fungi) in a bottle. Great White is awesome in my experience.
- Always use a shredded bark mulch layer on top of all your containers; this has a million benefits and no downsides. Avoid cedar and walnut products.
- Big Bloom by Fox Farm is great stuff, just like a concentrated tea full of highly nutritional microbeasty food.
- If you use coconut fiber, try the expanded Cocogro product by Botanicare. It's thoroughly rinsed for low low salts; a very important thing.
- Try keeping your lights at about 2 feet above plant tops, as this makes for super happy plants.
- LED lights are badass for sprouting and vegging, I love them and they run cool.
- Use 400 watt HID lights rather than 1000 watt due to several reasons of convenience.
- I would always recommend using Eye Blue Metal Halide Bulbs for flowering at the time of writing, and I have been a huge fan of these bulbs for almost a decade.

CHAPTER 6

Additives

Large and small nugget sized perlite

The notable dry additives and elements in a living TLO soil mix are many, but I want to run through several of them here to give you a better idea of why I use specific things. This section should help you wrap your head around what does what, for how long, and how quickly; this will be advantageous should you decide you want to substitute ingredients in your soil. Also, understanding many of these things will really open your eyes as to how things work in the natural world. It sure opened mine and continues to amaze me at every new turn. Again I want to strongly encourage you to do this my way (at least the first couple times) and not wing it. This will give you a proven working formula, and if you want to alter things in the future, make those changes slowly, one at a time; small moves.

Great White is a fantastic brand of myco fungi and has never let me down

The difference between granular and powdered forms of additives is important to note, and usually is directly relative to strength of release and length of release. There are several issues when growing TLO-style where this will matter a lot and I will strive to point all those out to you as we cover them.

Perlite

Perlite is, simply put, a volcanic glass that is all natural and quite solid in nature. When heated, this glass expands big time, resulting in the highly porous and light material called perlite. This material does not decompose or otherwise break down easily, which makes it perfect for aerating a living TLO soil mix. I would be lost trying to use a living soil mix in containers without perlite. I recommend using small nugget sized perlite due to the increased surface area, making it a much more effective aerating amendment.

I like to use perlite in any soil mix I am using in containers. When using living mixes in container growing, you always need to be highly concerned with making sure there is enough air for all the microlife to breathe AND enough for the plant roots as well. Please always use a respirator when mixing perlite; the dust can cause a really bad cough if inhaled. It's not toxic in any way, just an irritant. I always open the bag and spray a bit of water inside, just to cut down on the dust as much as possible.

Be very careful using bat guano as too much can quickly sizzle your plants

I Just want to note here that you really don't need perlite for outdoor mixes in raised beds or otherwise in the ground. The earth aerates itself quite well with all the life moving through it constantly. But in containers, perlite is (amazingly) perfect for aerating a living soil mix and it is usually fairly easy to find. As a second choice here you could use vermiculite; it is not quite as good as perlite for aeration used alone, but it works alright. Vermiculite holds a lot of water as well, so you could blend a mix of 50/50 of perlite/vermiculite resulting in great aeration and additional water retention.

Note: I highly recommend using a 50/50 blend of perlite/vermiculite to replace all pure perlite additions given in this book.

Basic Rule of Thumb for Using Perlite when TLO Container Growing

Keep in mind I have a worm farm and I add perlite to my worm food. Also, once you are recycling, most of your perlite will cycle through still intact—we *love* that—so your perlite additions will drop. Any time you aren't seeing plenty of recycled perlite in whatever soil you are mixing for containers, add 10-15% of the total soil mix volume of perlite. Air and perlite are VERY IMPORTANT TLO facets. Make a note on your calendar to check your perlite situation every six months or so. This problem can creep up on you slowly and will be imperceptible unless you are looking for it.

Mycorrhizal Fungus

Myco fungus, as I call it, is one of the most important parts of container growing in my experience—if you want the best buds. You need to know just a few things about this amazing fungus to use it successfully in TLO, and the first is the expiration date! Be sure to get a high-quality, fresh product here. When dormant and dry in bottles they are 100% good for around two years, and in soil mixes they are also good for at least a year as long as the bags of myco-infused soil mix have not been stored in direct sunlight or high heat for months. There are two main types of myco fungus, and these are the "ecto" (ectomycorrhizal fungi) and "endo" (endomycorrhizal fungi) types. Simply put, the ecto type of myco fungus mostly associates with tree roots, while the endo type associates with vegetables, other plants and cannabis. The term "arbuscular mycorrhizal fungus" (AMF), is also used, and refers to a type of endo myco fungus. The fundamental differences between the two types is that the ecto tends to "sheath" around the roots with its spider web-like hyphae growth, while the endo/AMF actually penetrates the

| REV'S TIP | The age of your bottled or bagged myco fungi is a big deal, because they only stay 100% viable for about two years as I understand it. Also, if stored at above 80°F, the shelf life will be shortened even more. I use the Great White brand dry soluble powder exclusively these days for my myco needs. |

cells of living roots, forming a symbiotic relationship with the plant.

Myco fungi that is dormant in the bottle (for sale) is pretty easy to find at high-end nurseries, online or in grow shops. It comes in both granular and soluble dry forms and is actually reasonably priced for what it does for you. Your yields and overall quality levels are greatly increased when this fungus is used in TLO container growing. The myco fungus is known as a mutalistic fungus, and it actually works with the plant. The roots supply the fungi with certain elements, and in turn the fungus actually brings available minerals and elements to the plant, effectively extending the reach of the roots. Not only can these myco fungi bring in nutrient elements, they can actually free locked-up nutrients, such as phosphorus (P), in the soil and bring them in an avail-

Collection of TLO additives organized on a shelf

able state to the plant roots. P is über-important to both root growth and size of flowers/yields, so you can see how important it is to have these myco fungi on the scene in your containers. I use only the Great White myco product these days. In a living and evolving supernatural soil mix, you only need to use this product one time during the entire life of any plant, and only at the very beginning of its life. I use it on sprouts as soon as they break ground, and on freshly rooted clones immediately after they are planted in soil for the first time.

Soluble applications of myco fungus should be delivered using chlorine-free water only. I used to use the granular version in the container just below where I set the root ball down, and I actually set the root ball down on a thin sprinkling of this granular version; this also works well. Whenever I transplant freshly rooted clones, I use a bagged myco fungi–infused soil mix, and my favorite for this purpose is the Gardner & Bloome (G&B) brand of Blue Ribbon Potting Soil. This is great soil, and it only needs to be aerated with a little additional perlite.

Blood Meal, Feather Meal and Guanos

These are high-nitrogen, dry, all natural fertilizers and I use all of them in TLO container growing. Cannabis likes a lot of nitrogen, and so does the living soil mix. A notable difference in those elements is the

PHOTO: IAN C.

A few of my favorite dry guanos

strength and length of release. The guanos (from either birds or bats) and the blood meal are both very strong and supply a lot of nitrogen fast. The feather meal has a much weaker release rate, but lasts *very* long in the soil mix. Why does this matter? First of all, you have to be very careful using blood meal and guanos because these are so powerful in any kind of soil mix; in fact, they can overdose your poor plants into a burned brown mess in no time if used improperly. The feather meal is a great fertilizer, and supplies slower nitrogen over a much longer time, along with some calcium. The combination of nitrogen and calcium is one that's much loved by TLO growers, and you'll come to see why. You could sub out hoof or horn meal, hair or fur, for feather meal, as long as the source animal is healthy; when using fur make sure the animal is free from things like Advantage flea treatments. Human hair is all good as long as it has not been dyed or treated.

Blood meal brings in a real big punch of nitrogen and supplies good iron along with a bunch of micronutrients and trace elements. You could sub out bird or bat guano for blood meal, like a 9-3-1 N-P-K guano, but you would be missing the rich iron and other vitamins/minerals in the blood meal. This lack of iron can be compensated for to a good degree with additional ratios of greensand. Release rates of blood meal are often thought to be slower than I suggest. Trust me, in a supernatural TLO soil mix your blood meal additions are consumed and processed much more rapidly than in a typical all natural soil mix without extra aeration, high nutrient levels, or elevated root/soil mix metabolism rates.

I am a big fan of using blood meal, not that I like the industry it comes from, but more like its all natural history on this planet. Blood is always a virtual stackhouse of prime power nutrients in a very concentrated dose, and plants have been living off the remains of dead animals forever. In nature nothing goes to waste, so omitting blood meal would not be on the TLO path for me, but it might be for you. Do your own research too; I have been growing and using blood meal for a very long time, and I have never even *heard* of anyone getting hurt from "bad" blood meal. Seems like some kind of bad hype synthetic fertilizer corporations would want to start, eh?

Feather meal is one of my all time favorite amendments and it brings both nitrogen and calcium (Ca) to the game; microbeasties are all about their N and Ca! However this form of nitrogen is far different from that of blood meal (derived from a totally different protein) and is the common protein (N form) found in hair, hoofs, horns and feathers. The nitrogen in feather meal is slow-release, and so much harder for the microbeasties to access. This makes it a primo element especially for flowering (and *long* flowering) cannabis plants that you want to keep happy in smaller container sizes. The proper use of this amendment can greatly affect yield so I would get some if I were you.

A final note on guanos: Don't use these fresh out of the birds or bats, or else you will most likely kill your plants. Be very careful if collecting dry guano from bats or birds. Some dangerous things can be lurking, including a few types of fungi that are very nasty to humans. Always use a respirator, and be sure to compost the guano first. It must be cooked (composted) before it is safely usable in container growing.

Bone Meal Vs Steamed Bone Meal

Steamed or un-steamed bone meal? When using it for spikes, layering or as an addition to recycled soil mixes, this makes no difference that I have ever been able to discern. Bone meal is a wicked good source of calcium, phosphorus and some slow release nitrogen along with a ton of other micros and trace elements. It also works as a buffering element due to the high levels of calcium, and in your soil mixes (Supernatural or Recycled blends in this book) feel free to use steamed or unsteamed bone meal.

Lime and Dolomite Lime

I have noticed that the lime stuff tends to perplex many new TLO growers, so let me break it down to you from a TLO perspective. Dry lime in your mix serves several purposes in TLO growing. I use two grades

My powdered dolomite lime
storage containers of choice
next to a measuring cup

of Dolomite lime: a granular, fast-acting, prilled type, and a powdered type. Prilled is just like granular, except it is more soluble, hence its fast-acting nature. Some granular Dolomite lime is just like small rocks and has very little power to influence pH or supply nutrient elements quickly, due to its dense state. Prilled Dolomite lime (sometimes called pelletized lime) has a soluble shell around small Dolomite lime granules, and it works really well.

Hydrated lime should be completely avoided. Due to its extreme power it can easily kill life and take pH into deadly high ranges (like 11.0-ish) for your plants. Dolomite lime gives the plants magnesium and calcium as well as buffering pH from dropping too low or getting too high. You should have plenty of magnesium available to your plants, especially during flowering, but too much magnesium can really turn out harsh in your smoke. It can also lock up your soil mix into a cement-like state, starving everything in it for airflow and turning the soil mix structure to shit, so make sure you stay on top of your magnesium additions. Cannabis likes a *lot* of magnesium, but like everything else you can go too far, especially using things like Sul-Po-Mag (also known as KMag), which is very powerful stuff. I do not use this stuff. However, you could if you wanted to, and if you felt that your plants needed it. There's heavy potassium in KMag as well, so just take note that this could be a very deadly addition if you use too much.

I recommend that you use two types of Dolomite lime in TLO container growing, both powdered and prilled. Make sure the prilled Dolomite lime says "fast acting" on it, so as not to get it confused with granular (hard rock) Dolomite lime.

Greensand and Azomite

In my opinion, greensand is a major player in TLO container growing, and I really loves my Azomite too. These are both HUGE regarding remineralization of your recycling soil!

Greensand's chemical makeup is approximately as follows:
- Iron (Fe) 12-19%
- Potassium (K) 5-7%
- Silicon (Si) 25%
- Oxygen (O) 45%
- Magnesium (Mg) 2-3%
- Aluminum (Al) 2%
- Sodium (Na) 0.25%
- Hydrogen (H) 0.47%

Greensand also contains over 30 other trace minerals and micronutrients—so as you can see, this is some kick ass stuff for all natural cannabis growing. In supernatural TLO cannabis growing it is pure magic. It affects soil structure for better aeration, and the benefits go well beyond what scientific research knows, I would bet. Try very hard to source this wonderful addition. Make a special brain-note of the iron levels that greensand brings to the game.

Azomite has a broad spectrum of over 70 metabolically active minerals and trace elements. It is also reported to increase yields and impart cold-heartiness to plants along with favorable electro-chemical (CEC) properties for the soil. I use this stuff both in micronized (powdered) and granular forms. Here are just *some* of the good things Azomite brings to the table for TLO growing, chemically speaking:
- Boron (B)
- Calcium (Ca)
- Chlorine (Cl)
- Cobalt (Co)
- Copper (Cu)
- Iron (Fe)
- Magnesium (Mg)
- Molybdenum (Mo)
- Nitrogen (N)
- Phosphorus (P)
- Potassium (K)
- Silicon (Si)
- Sulfur (S)

Greensand is essential for a TLO grow running to its full potential

When making your first Supernatural Soil Mix Recipe 2.2, I would use the powdered version, and I would use the granular for all recycled mixes that followed. Good stuff, Maynard!

Ground oyster shell

Oyster Shells

You'll hear me talking about calcium a lot, and rightly so. It is one of the most important elements when TLO growing in a living soil mix. I treat calcium much more like a primary nutrient than a secondary nutrient. Not only do oyster shell products bring calcium to the TLO soil mixes, they are also responsible for creating a very bacteria-friendly soil mix. Now, there are a few grades of these processed oyster shells. One is almost in a powder form, and this is called "oyster shell flour" by some brands and nurseries. Another form is called "crushed oyster shell" and it is in smaller pieces about the size of a dime. These small pieces are like little artificial reefs in the ocean in many ways. The oyster shell surface is very porous and buffers the pH upwards; those are two very bacteria-friendly things right there. The pH is only affected in the direct vicinity of the oyster shell pieces. This is wonderful news for the fungi,

---

REV'S TIP You have to search a bit for oyster shell products sometimes. I love the Down to Earth brand of ground oyster shell. Since I live on the coast I also have access to crushed oyster shell, which is just a very coarse grade (small pieces) version of ground shell. This stuff is fantastic for several reasons; it's pH balancing, the bacteria just seem to go crazy with this stuff in the mix and the worms love it too! I would go out of my way to find this stuff, or get a local nursery to order some for you.

which can grow through the soil mix mostly avoiding the oyster shell pieces. The other grade of oyster shell is called "ground oyster shell" and it is basically the consistency of course sand.

Much like phosphorus (and all other mineral elements particularly), calcium must be released more slowly to match the speed at which the roots can actually absorb it. The goal in TLO is not to cram nutrients down the plants' throats. Too much calcium, or phosphorus, or anything else, basically, is a bad thing. You normally cannot "fix" problems by just pouring more of any particular additive into your plants' containers. It is best to provide the calcium in TLO from multiple sources, like bone meal, feather meal, lime and oyster shell. The composition of oyster shell is basically 95% calcium carbonate, about 3.5% silicate and with other trace elements like, glycine, calcium phosphate, zinc, manganese, aluminum, etc. Last but not least, from everything I have read and peeps I have talked to in the oyster farming biz, oyster farming seems to have a hugely positive impact on the environment.

Soft Rock Phosphate and Rock Phosphate

Don't blow off the soft rock phosphate (SRP) and rock phosphate (RP) in your mix. These two things (RP and SRP) are essentially the same mineral in different grades. I like to use the SRP, the powdered form,

when mixing some of my own soil mixes involving lime and high nitrogen. The SRP has a sort of magical (magical to me at any rate) effect on a soil mix when a lot of powerful nitrogen like blood meal and/or bird/bat guanos, are blended with lime (calcium). Normally, you would lose some nitrogen in a gas (ammonia) form from the chemical reaction here. However, the SRP keeps the nitrogen in the soil mix rather than allowing it to float away as ammonia gas. It also allows the calcium to "stick" to the soil mix instead of leaching out due to electromagnetic properties (CEC) of the SRP.

Organic rock phosphate
promotes root growth

PHOTO: MONICA GRIFFIN

I use both granular rock phosphate and powdered SRP in my soil mixes, and SRP or RP is going to be a very important part of yours as well. The microbeasties seriously love their nitrogen and calcium. I'll say that again: the microbeasties inside your soil mix, the little living things that make TLO growing work absolutely love nitrogen and calcium. You would do well to tattoo that on the inside of your eyelids so you'll be reminded of it even when you're asleep, and it is why I keep banging you on the head with it. I use rock phosphate as well because I recycle my soil mix. If you are not planning on recycling your soil mix, then the use of granular RP is optional, at best.

SRP & RP is just a great, phosphorus-filled mineral element, and it is pretty available to the plant, as phosphorus goes. It possesses boron and silicon, to name just two of the 60 or so trace elements it has. I love this stuff and I try and get it in the smallest particle size possible. Micronized is my favorite grade of this, and as you will see in my custom soil mixes, a little bit of this goes a long way in container growing.

RP is absolutely a must have if recycling and you can option out to only using this in granular form once you have recycled your soil once. I use the micronized SRP these days mostly very lightly in teas. But when mixing your first Supernatural Soil Mix Recipe 2.2, I would use the powdered version (SRP) if at all possible. Use at least one of them in every new or recycled mix. I even add RP to my worm food in small amounts.

Humic Acid Ore A.K.A. Humic Shale Ore is a really nice addition and I use it in very small amounts; I just love the results I saw from using a little bit in a few side by side comparisons of my own years ago. I know it is listed as optional, and it is, but I would highly recommend it. It contains something like 70+ trace elements, and is 45% humic acid (ore). This stuff is very ancient, and if your water source is a little bit higher in PPM, or for some reason you have some building up of salty minerals in your soil mix, the addition of this amendment in slightly higher ratios will do well to counter these negative effects. It seems to be a primo bio-stimulant, and in the shale/ore form the humic acid levels are not crazy available like they would be in any liquid forms. We never, ever, OD our soil mix with organic acids, and in the supernatural TLO processes all the good organic acids are created and accessed at

Humic acid ore

rates according to environmental needs via the microbeasties and their associated activities in the soil. Like anything else, don't overdo it with this one, as it is a very potent addition.

Dried Fish

I really like this product by Seagate and because when I read the ingredients it says, "made from 16 pounds of dried fish and nothing else." Bingo! I don't really ever add this to my soil mixes because the cost is prohibitive to me, but it works great in spikes, and for layering and especially for top dressing plants just going into flowering. The dried fish runs 11-5-1 as far as N-P-K values go, and the P is

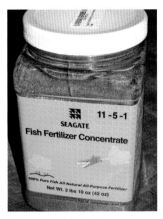

Dried Fish by Seagate

bonded up pretty good in the calcium so it won't release too much P available on the scene too quickly. This turns out badly if it happens in a living soil mix with living roots present. This is also great for use in teas in place of liquid fish fertilizers. Use this one sparingly as it packs a pretty big punch!

Notable liquid TLO friendly all natural nutrients are very important to know about. Many liquids that are actually all organic and even some that fly OMRI ratings are counter productive in TLO growing, because they either kill or piss off the microlife, due to pH swings and unnatural availability of powerful nutrients, such as phosphorus and nitrogen, and organic acids, such as humic, fulvic, phosphoric, citric, etc. I keep the liquids very simple in TLO, so let's just go over what I use, when and why. This way my experience can guide you here at first, because trust me *mis amigos,* you DO NOT want to casually pour some kind of sneaky synthetic liquid into your pristine TLO soil mix, lest disasters ensue! Your primary mission when TLO growing is to NOT use anything with any synthetic salts in it, dry or liquid. *Any* synthetic nutrient salt kills microbial life once the soil starts to dry out, and keeps the soil mix inhospitable to the beneficial microbeasties as well. Unnaturally high levels of organic acids will throw microbeasty land into chaos and they will not be able to perform supernaturally for a couple of weeks following. You can see how this would suck big time for a plant, during flowering *especially.*

This cal mag product contains synthetic nutrients and should NOT be used in a TLO grow

Organic Acids

In many organic liquids these acids are used for the same reasons synthetic salts are used. Organic acids like phosphoric acid and things like sulfur are often used as long-term preservatives in liquid organic fertilizer products. Organic acids, like phosphoric, fulvic, humic and ascorbic acids chelate nutrients, similar to how synthetic salts chelate nutrients. For our purposes, chelating nutrients means making those nutrients *very* absorbable to the roots; I would argue it is actually more like force feeding. Mother Nature and the plants know what they need and when they need it. In TLO growing, we put the plant in charge of choosing which nutrients it wants by allowing it to interact with the microbial life in the soil mix, the way plants have been doing it for millions of years. Drastic pH swings caused by these organic acids basically gives the microlife the microbial version of The Bends, just like SCUBA divers get. Both the microlife and scuba divers suffer when there's a drastic change in the density of their environment, way too fast. Anything that messes with the soil mix microbial life will cause the plant uptake problems shortly thereafter. You can recover from a moderate organic acids error, but the synthetic salts will continue to inhibit and kill microbial life in the soil.

Organic acids are all well and good, but liquid nutrient products that have high amounts of these acids should be used with great care, and I recommend avoiding them completely in TLO growing philosophy, *especially* the products that are straight humic, and/or fulvic acid. True Living Organics lets life do what it does best, not usually how humans think it should be done. Force feeding is not the way to the highest quality harvest in my experience, and that's the real deal with this book. This will guide you to the finest quality smoke that can be had; to me, TLO bud is equal to or greater than all other contenders in quality, and I have smoked a lot of cannabis. Once you have used a good dose of something heavy with organic acid(s) on your soil mix, you may be stuck having to use that on a regular basis, if your soil mix doesn't repopulate quickly

---

REV'S TIP Controlling pH in TLO growing is rarely a concern. Balancing and buffering your soil mix, along with using a pure, consistent water source, makes all that pH stuff basically irrelevant. Liquid mineral supplements usually raise the pH, but not always; and things like 100% grape juice and lemon juice lower the pH drastically. Doing this can have detrimental effects on the microbeasties, so I hardly ever concern myself with the pH of liquids, because I rarely use anything but water and organic teas, which I will tell you about later in this book.

and reach equilibrium. Just like the nutrient companies love!

The whole world—hell the whole universe—works from chelation to some degree; this degree is an all natural occurrence in nature and not out of any bottle. When you tweak the levels of chelating elements in TLO growing you are acting counterproductively to your ultimate goal. Soil life will get hurt, and then quality will then also get hurt. Stay supernatural and see what happens.

Liquid Calcium and Cal-Mag Products

I used to use CaMg+ by General Organics consistently in my water for the sake of convenience. I use it at a ratio of 10 - 15 drops per gallon of reverse osmosis water. It is very important not to overdo it with any mineral liquids. If you shop around for one of these types of liquid mineral supplements, make sure there isn't something like iron added, because that likely means there are synthetic salts (called EDTA) present and these will wreak havoc on your soil/plant health. Look in the "derived from" part of the label. There are also dry powdered (soluble) versions of calcium/magnesium products available, just make SURE they are all naturally sourced.

I have warned you before, and I will warn you again: Maintaining good magnesium levels is a skill in TLO growing. Cannabis likes a lot of magnesium, especially in flowering, but too much is very bad. As you acquire TLO skills, having available magnesium in your soil mix from multiple sources will be easy. My CaMg+ additions bring in additional calcium and magnesium on a consistent basis, and all my plants love it.

I have grown very successful TLO crops using CaMg+ by General Organics, with reverse osmosis filtered water, and using about 15 drops per gallon (or until about 60-90 PPM on a TDS meter) every time I watered, or fed with a tea.

General Organics CaMg+ works great in TLO growing

This particular product has a 5:1 (five to one) ratio of calcium to magnesium, which in my opinion is awesome for cannabis growing. Choosing whether or not to use this kind of product will depend a lot on the mineral value of your chosen TLO soil mix, but if you are using a pure water source, you may benefit greatly from dialing in a certain level of this type product every, watering.

Super naturally healthy TLO growth from fish-based tea

Fish Fertilizer and Fox Farm's Big Bloom

Oh man, these used to be my favorite TLO liquids of all time! To me the fish fertilizer and the Big Bloom are both acceptable in teas, in lower ratios than recommended on the bottles. Both the Big Bloom and fish fertilizer are full of organic matter that you can actually see! In fact, when watering with either of these present, I tend to stir up the solution between plants, to make sure they all get equal amounts of the organic matter, because the matter will actually start to settle faster than you might think. This can cause an unequal distribution of the matter, and the same can happen with teas, so keep this well in mind and stir up your solution between plant feedings.

Take extra special note of the N-P-K (0.01-0.3-0.7) numbers on the Big Bloom. This is very important if you are subbing something out for it. These über-low numbers are what it is all about, and the microlife loves this stuff! Now don't go thinking that all Fox Farm liquid fertilizers are this natural, because they are not. Big Bloom is special, and fairly suited to TLO growing conditions, as long as you use it sparingly in teas only. You will notice the level of phosphorus (0.3) is less than half of the potassium (0.7) in the Big Bloom. This is great for TLO since you have the spikes and the layers in which you can deliver higher phosphorus from sources such as guanos and bone meal. Potassium is every bit as important as phosphorus during flowering, and at any stage of growth for that matter. In indoor growing environments, the plants tend to transpire (breathe) a lot at high metabolism rates. This will very often create a need for greater potassium (K) availability near the roots. I would recommend having some Big Bloom on your shelves if at all possible.

As I understand it there are some fairly high levels of sodium chloride (basically sea salt) in this product, so this needs to be considered. I use this product very sparingly and only once in a tea during the first three weeks of flowering. I believe the product uses the salts as a preservative to increase shelf life. When I use it in a tea I use it at a ratio of about 1 or 2 tablespoons per gallon of tea. It is very hard (impossible for me) to find a liquid fish that has not been bombed with phosphoric acid and or sulfur as preservative agents.

I no longer use any liquid fish products. Instead I use the dried fish by Seagate. However, should you choose to use a liquid fish product in your teas we should examine some of these liquid fishy fertilizers. Fish fertilizer liquids vary quite a bit in their N-P-K values, and this should be a consideration. My favorite fish fertilizer N-P-K ratio is 5-1-1, for high-power growth teas in smaller containers. 3-3-0.3 is also a great combination, and this one is especially useful with longer flowering sativas and sativa dominant strains in smaller containers. Mixing some kelp (liquid seaweed) and fish emulsion works as a fairly decent all natural, all purpose nutrient addition to a tea. Never mix liquid nutrients with other liquid nutrients without water, as that can lockout nutrients before they ever get on the scene! Always mix liquid nutrients in water. Molasses is another great thing to mix with fish fertilizers in teas, as they complement each other in a great way! Be very careful when selecting liquid fish fertilizers, and as always be extra wary of anything with added iron, or "Organic Based" or "All Organic Based" and try using dried fish instead.

Big Bloom by Fox Farm is very TLO friendly

As I mentioned above, several popular liquid fish fertilizers have high levels of either phosphoric acid or sulfur in them as a preservative to increase shelf life. Try to avoid these types if possible, and make sure the P value comes from the fish bones and not from the addition of liquid phosphoric acid. Dry fish and fish meal are both excellent in teas and stay fresh practically forever. So use liquid fish if you must, but I recommend using dried fish or fish meal instead.

Molasses

Molasses has an N-P-K ratio of around 1-0-5, so not that much is needed. In teas I usually use about 2 teaspoons and every now and then up to 1 tablespoon per gallon of bubbling tea. I never use molasses outside of teas. It also helps other nutrients to be absorbed by plant roots by means of mild chelation. Make sure you use the "unsulfured" version of molasses, and I recommend those that are overtly organic; make sure it says ALL natural or organic. Black-strap molasses is awesome, and is my preferred type. It's just a bit tougher to find, but if it's not readily available where you are, either kind of molasses works fine.

Molasses has an N-P-K ratio of around 1-0-5, so not that much is needed

Care should be taken during the second half of flowering when using a lot of molasses in teas. The high magnesium value of molasses, which is one of its great assets, can be detrimental to the smoking qualities of the final product. Just be aware of this, because any leftover magnesium will be stored in your buds and can make the smoke a bit hot, compared to properly finished buds. Cannabis loves her magnesium, so a lot has to be available to her throughout growth and especially in flowering. Molasses is a great way to provide this, but like anything else, you don't want to use too much. Spring, well, and city tap/municipal water is normally high in totally dissolved magnesium and calcium levels too, so be careful if using those together.

The ONLY liquids I use in my TLO gardens are CaMg+, molasses and a little Big Bloom. The Big Bloom is totally optional in teas, and I use it just to kick up the flowering responses in the plant and for convenience, at low ratios, sometimes. But it won't destroy your supernatural grow if you use some quality liquid fish in your teas.

PRODUCTS THAT ARE NOT TLO-FRIENDLY

Not all products are TLO-friendly. Your biggest enemy here will be synthetic salts, which are often just listed as a few capital letters like EDTA on plant fertilizer. These salts will really kill a TLO container soil mix fast, so avoid these types of salts! There are synthetic salts in both liquid and dry amendments. Also, there are other salts that are bad because of the levels of them in certain products, and especially coconut coir products. Sea salt is certainly all OMRI (Organic Materials Review Institute) good, but too much of it is not good for a TLO grow in the same way that too much is not good for you.

Here is a partial list of common products that should NEVER be used in a TLO grow:

- Liquid, Tiger Bloom or Grow Big by Fox Farm (synthetic salts)
- Dry, American Pride or Marine Cuisine by Fox Farm (synthetic salts)
- Hot Shots No Pest Strips (poisonous big time)
- Avid or Floramite (poisonous big time)
- Sulfur burners (poisonous and harshes out your smoke big time)
- Liquid, Earth Juice fertilizers (too high in organic –chelating- acids)
- Liquid, soaps or oils like Neem oil entering the soil mix from run off treating bugs or mold.
- Generally speaking almost all of Advanced Nutrients products are hostile to TLO style (synthetic salts)
- Generally speaking almost all of Botanicare products are hostile to TLO style (synthetic salts)
- Softened water (way high salt content)
- Hard water (way high salt content)
- Chlorinated water (chloramine is the super chlorine in most city water these days)
- Super Thrive
- Liquid Karma
- CalMag Plus by Botanicare (synthetic salts)
- pH-Up or pH-Down products, period

CHAPTER 7

Watering and Feeding

Water reservoir for a TLO grow

Water sources and filtering options are very important considerations when TLO growing, and a whole bunch of people already growing organically could likely get a huge boost in quality and yields if they were aware of just how important this whole subject is. City tap or municipal water is the biggest potential problem when growing with a living soil mix. Filtering this type of water is actually fairly simple, and I will share my favorite sources for water filtration. My favorite brand for this in the USA is called Pure Water Products. More about them and their filters later, but for now suffice it to say that your water source is a huge deal when growing TLO or any organic style. If you use well, spring, or tap/city water, then you really want to filter it for a number of reasons.

City, well and spring water all have some potentially bad things in common. Often they are "hard," which means they contain a lot of dissolved magnesium and calcium, etc. This type of water will accumulate salts (magnesium, calcium, et al.) around the root zones (rhizosphere) altering the pH drastically over the course of a month or two, and making the area inhospitable to some of the key microbeasties. It seems to me to really mess with the mycorrhizal fungus, so things like phosphorus can then tend to lock out in the soil mix without the aid of the mighty myco fungi. Another big downside is the seasonally changing ratios of various dissolved mineral salts in any underground aquifer, along with *who*

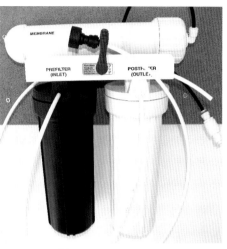

A tabletop reverse osmosis filtering unit Rev loves

knows what else from local plumbing, and other sources. Every once in a while, spring or well water will be perfect for growing all TLO style, because of low ratios of dissolved salts, and a nice balance of them as well. City tap water almost always has huge problems, including all those that spring and well water usually have.

Note: After I started learning just how much spooky crap is in public municipal (tap) water—well, let me put it like this: At the time of writing, we don't cook with or drink tap water. In fact, we haven't done for about five years. We filter all our water using an R/O machine; my dogs and cats don't drink tap water. I just get a case of Arrowhead spring water that us peeps usually drink and the animals get filtered water. Sound extreme? Maybe you should look into this yourselves—just sayin'.

REV'S TIP River and stream water is normally good to use outdoors when growing plants in the earth, but you should check it with a TDS meter to make sure it is not too high in dissolved mineral salts. A reading below 100 PPM is almost always fine even when container growing. River and stream water (in fact any groundwater source from the aquifer) should be checked for unknown possibilities like pollution, including the existence of bad microbial life, and organic chemical elements out of balance. Rivers and streams especially, but even well aquifers can have some nasty stuff in them, thanks to people or companies nearby—Up Aquifer.

This carbon filtering unit removes chloramine among other things

City/municipal tap water these days is almost always disinfected with a chemical called "chloramine"—which is, simply stated, a very stable form of chlorine that you cannot simply bubble or even boil out of the water. This is hazardous to your soil mix in a huge way! Activated carbon filtering is the way to deal with this chloramine issue, and carbon filtering will also remove much more potential nastiness from your city water. Fluoride interferes with over 30 natural plant processes, and can definitely mess up germination rates. Reverse osmosis filters will handle the fluoride; carbon filters cannot, just so you know.

Well water is tricky, and I have seen TLO plants thriving when well water is running about 150 PPM. On the flip side I have seen bad results trying to use 80 PPM well water with TLO container growing. It's all about those PPM values. Our TLO soil mixes can adapt to a lot of different situations, including different water types, but only if the PPM values of the water are balanced and somewhat consistent, and of course, not toxic—duh! Some of the very common issues well and spring water have are things like too much iron, magnesium, manganese and sulfur—or any combination of those. Not to mention a plethora of other (even toxic) things like pollutants.

"Waste" water from your reverse osmosis unit is useful. When you use your reverse osmosis water filter (R/O filter) you will generate a huge amount of "waste water." Here's the dealio with that.

This water is not poison, or toxic in any way. It is simply your source water (before the R/O filtering unit) at about double the PPM value. If you run two carbon filters in your R/O unit along with the R/O membrane as I recommend, and you filter city tap water, this waste water will also be chlorine/chloramine free, but will still have some crap in it like fluoride. I myself use this to water trees and veggies in the ground outdoors; you could also cook with it, like boiling potatoes or whatever. If your source water is from a well or spring that is not chlorinated, and you feel confident about the salts/minerals that are dissolved in it, you could use some of it to cut back into your pure filtered water to raise your PPM value up to between 70-90 PPM and you should be all good.

People who say "water is water" don't know what the hell they are talking about. Your water source is a powerful and fundamental part of any garden, so make sure you handle this out of the gate and you will have far fewer problems; *word*.

Watering Twice

Arguably one of the most important fundamental practices in TLO container growing is watering twice. This can have a huge influence on root health as well as mineral absorption. Here's how it works: You water with plain water, lightly, until you see some water run out the bottom of the container. Then wait for at least 30 minutes (I often wait a couple hours) then water again until you see good drainage from the bottom. This evenly saturates the container soil mix and the roots. If you do not do this, the roots will actually start guiding the water flow through the container and you will end up with dry spots that are bad for roots, and bad for plants, especially when container growing! Calcium issues often ensue shortly after the dry spots are created.

I like to have trays underneath my containers so that any water that drains out initially gets sucked back up into the soil mix through the process of capillary action. There's no need to flush when growing TLO-style in containers, unless you are prone to using high PPM water, or you go and add something you shouldn't have. Higher TDS/PPM levels like the ones found in city tap, well and spring water will accumulate salts around the root zones of the plants, and will end up "strangling" them if you don't do regular flushing.

To avoid watering twice you can make a couple of moves. You can use the self-watering containers like I do; boom, simple. You can also measure how much water your particular flowering containers use and suck back up within 30 minutes from the catch trays. Water one of these pots with enough water to fill up the catch tray totally, then wait 30 minutes and measure how much water is leftover then subtract that from however much water you initially poured on the plant, and bingo! You have a good guideline for how much water to give each plant so it gets fully watered and has no levels of standing water for more than 30-40 minutes.

Watering Self-Watering Containers in TLO

I will sometimes just fill the bottom tray full of good water when watering, under a few circumstances:

If I'm not sure they need a full watering yet but I will be away all day. During very hot days this is a good safety move.

During the last 10 days before harvest I just fill their tray when needed with pure R/O filtered water with no CaMg+ or anything added.

Sometimes I will do a normal full watering on them from the top and about 15 minutes later I will top off the lower tray filling it to max. This is handy when very large plants are in pretty small containers during hot days.

Otherwise I water them normally from the top most of the time, in order to catalyze all the TLO action up in the top of the soil mix in the containers, giving all the microlife and the roots some moisture. I always have a tray or two of frozen good water in ice cube trays in my freezer, and I use these on any super hot days right after watering. I plunk down an ice cube in their lower trays to help keep them cool; they love this!

> **REV'S TIP** You should learn how much water it takes to water the plant in self-watering containers and have the tray mostly fill up afterwards; the 11-inch (about 2 gallons US DRY) self-watering pots, if they are dry, can easily hold 1600 ml of water (about 1.5 quarts US LIQUID) and not overflow at all but have some extra water in the catch tray, just how we like it.

Great Tabletop Reverse Osmosis and Carbon Filtering Units

Okay, no more Mr. Nice Guy—just get one of these and you will solve so many of your problems. If you have no water problems, then by all means, don't change anything, but if you do have problems, reverse osmosis filtering is likely much easier and cheaper than you anticipate it will be. A countertop reverse osmosis filtering unit (R/O filter) comes with three filtering chambers. Two are used for carbon filters, and one is the actual reverse osmosis membrane that removes dissolved salts/solids. First the water hits the pre (carbon) filter, then the R/O membrane, then the post (carbon) filter and mine makes about 1.5 gallons per hour. I get my filters from Pure Water Products, and these guys will set you up with a garden hose attachment free for the asking. I use their "Style A" countertop R/O Filtering Unit. I replace the pre carbon filter once every six months, and then both carbon filters once per year. The R/O membrane filter lasts for three years at least and is inexpensive and simple to replace.

> **REV'S TIP** Here's the link to Pure Water Products' website: www.pwgazette.com/. I use the Style A countertop Reverse Osmosis Machine, with a free garden hose attachment. I also have used their stand alone carbon filter units, which are designed to remove chlorine/chloramine from 20000 gallons of water. The filter cartridges are about $20 USD each. This is a good option if you are using well balanced city tap water with a low PPM of below 80 or so.

Here are a few great tips about how to use reverse osmosis units in order to get the most out of them for the longest time. First, get a TDS meter to see when you actually need to change your R/O membrane. Also see "Softened Water" in the Troubleshooting section of this book. (I would also normally recommend using some kind of sediment filter inline *before* the R/O unit.) If your water is "hard" and above, say, 170 PPM on a TDS meter, then you can install a water softening unit (inline BEFORE the R/O unit) to make your R/O Unit last

TLO-grown doobies are divine

Single carbon filters can work with low PPM water

much longer. NEVER use straight softened water on your plants; it will kill them! Put your carbon cartridge replacement schedule on a calendar, because this is another thing that will start to cause unhappy plants "out of nowhere" when in reality it is your carbon filters being too old to work well enough anymore.

Water pH and Water TDS/PPM

PPM stands for "Parts Per Million" and it is how your TDS (Totally Dissolved Salts/Solids) meter will display the readings it takes. After I use my R/O filtering unit on my city tap water, my TDS reading is about 10 PPM. For any water source that is 30 PPM or below you can probably get away with just using a carbon filter for chloramine removal. Also, the pH of the water is basically irrelevant (nominal) if the water is below 20 PPM. If TDS levels are above 80 PPM, the pH starts to matter to a *much* greater degree.

Let's use an example to explain this further. When you are outside in 50°F weather, it isn't warm, but it isn't a biggie at all. But if you were neck deep in 50°F water, you would have a *big* problem with cold! The same sort of thing applies for pH values related to your water's PPM levels. Air is less dense than water. 10 PPM water is less dense than 100 PPM water (the water in my example), so the effects of a denser "atmosphere" or environment are much more profound.

As your smoking appreciation becomes more and more sophisticated, your high-quality organic palate will be able to tell cannabis grown with pure water sources from cannabis grown using higher TDS/PPM water sources; hard to imagine perhaps, but absolutely true. Because of this, I always recommend pure water sources for TLO growing, and choosing rain, reverse osmosis, or distilled water will make everything that much

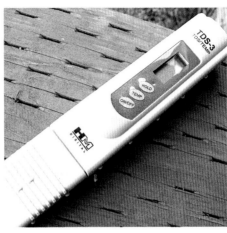

TDS meters are inexpensive and handy

smoother and raise the smoking quality to five star all the way! To really get a good idea of how elegant TLO grown cannabis smokes, I always recommend doobies. Glassware with resin from synthetic grown cannabis will really mess up your organic smoke, so don't screw yourself there and use a clean piece, or make it doobie-time!

I still love a good doobie these days, but within the last few years I have really gotten into vaping my TLO flowers using a portable vaporizer that I love: The PAX! I just can't begin to tell you how truly elegant and diverse all the different resin properties shine through when vaping with a quality vaporizer. More about the PAX later.

Hard Water and TLO Container Growing

Hard water is water that contains high levels of dissolved magnesium and calcium mineral salts, as I have said, not to mention whatever *else* is in your water—yikes. You can see the "scale" it leaves over time on your coffeemaker if you use city, well or spring water. This will also happen to your soil mix if you water your plants with hard water. The mineral salts will collect in the soil and around the root zones and build up, interfering with airflow through the soil, to the roots and to the microlife along with changing the pH in the rhizosphere. Don't try to get away with using hard water, or you may as well just accept the sub par results that will follow this water source choice.

Now on the flipside, if your tap/city water comes out of the faucet at (or below) say 60 PPM you may be able to get away with using an activated carbon filter (see the single carbon filter in the picture) to remove the chloramine. The trick here is to let the water flow slowly through the filter unit, because how effectively/thoroughly these elements are removed is determined by the length of time the water is in contact with the carbon filter. I also have used a dual version of the filter in the picture which allowed me to thoroughly remove the chloramine while also allowing me to run the water more quickly through the filters, and this comes in handy in larger grows.

Dehumidifier and Rainwater

Water collected by dehumidifiers is basically distilled water, and is fine to use in my experience as long as you keep the unit clean around the collection areas and especially the collection tray itself. Rainwater is my number one favorite to use in TLO growing, and if you have that option

Water collected by dehumidifiers is basically distilled water

then use it, you lucky devil! If you collect rainwater off your roof, do some checking into the type of roof you have, because there are types of shingles that will leach out chemicals into the rainwater. If your roof is all good, by all means set yourself up to collect the water from there into storage tanks under or above ground where the water can be stored while being aerated with air pumps.

There are many resourceful ways to collect rainwater, and when I was a guerrilla grower outdoors, we would even set up collectors made from tarps tied to trees. We would then fill buried waterbed mattresses. Where there's a will, there's a way! Rainwater is the best you can get in my opinion, and is full of all kinds of beneficial elements and even microbial life. I could devote a lot of pages to rainwater, but let's just say that this is the water you seek for the ultimate five star connoisseur buds, in my humble opinion. If I owned my own house I would for sure set up a rain collection system, but for now I use reverse osmosis water and get cannabis that smokes luxurious. So as long as your water source is a pure one, for the most part, your final product will be suited for the über-connoisseur!

REV'S TIP I can't say enough good things about rainwater. Like distilled water it is nominal in dissolved solids, and it also seems to contain microlife too; heavenly microlife! If I was using this water exclusively for TLO container growing I would almost always add about 10 - 15 drops per gallon of CaMg+ by General Organics to keep the slow and steady supply of calcium coming to the microlife and the plants, or I would adjust my lime ratios up slightly (15% or so) in my soil mixes, to use just rain water with no mineral amending.

Fresh Water Fish Tanks and TLO Growing

If your fresh water fish tank is all healthy and happy, and you don't add chemicals to remove chlorine or anything along those lines, your fresh-water fish tank water is like a giant organic tea, full of good available nutrients and *plenty* of microlife, and you should use a little bit of this water when brewing your own organic teas as a biocatalyst if you have the option; you can just *inoculate* your teas with a little aquarium water. You need to use reverse osmosis water to fill your tank, or very low TDS water, if you want to use this water in any real amounts very

Fresh water fish tanks, as long as they're healthy, are a great source of water that is rich in microlife!

> **REV'S TIP** If you have a healthy fish tank, no de-chlorinating or medical elements added, try using about 2 ounces of this fishy water per gallon of pure water every time you water, and I do this up until 2 weeks before harvest myself. It's magically good! Water was meant to be alive, my esteemed homeskillets.

often on your plants. If you don't, extraneous mineral salts will build up in the rhizosphere, causing problems. I have a 55-gallon freshwater fish tank full of guppies and a huge 10-year-old algae eater. I do water changes of 5 gallons once a month using reverse osmosis water. I never add any chemicals to my water and my fish have never been sick. The living dynamic in the fish tank is on a parallel with my TLO growing containers with plants in them. The soil mix is the water in this comparison, with the fish being the plants, and they both depend upon high levels of good microbial life and the absence of funky corporate driven chemicals.

Basically, if you have a healthy freshwater fish tank, the water in it is mega-full of good microlife! It can also be added to teas, as a biocatalyst as I said above. I add fishy water to my teas at a rate of 1oz per gallon of bubbling tea, and I do this about every other time I make a tea. The picture of the aquarium salts shows you exactly what I add to my own fish tank—because I use pure filtered water for my fish as well—at a ratio of about 1 tablespoon per 10 gallons of reverse osmosis water, and my fish are as healthy as my cannabis plants.

Using Water With Nutrient Elements That Stay Suspended

Here's a nice little trick that I use from time to time. Certain guanos, insect frass, my dried fish meal, micronized Azomite, Humes Gardening Blend and alfalfa meal are several examples of things you can use, mixed in very small amounts, directly in your water *just* before using that water. Sometimes between flowering teas, I will just use about 1/8th of a teaspoon per plant of Fox Farm's High P Bat Guano 0-5-0 for N-P-K values. This guano is finely graded and stays suspended in the water, allowing you to use it globally—albeit lightly—in your water. *Do not do this regularly* or it *will* go south on you, but every now and then it can give you a little bump up, if you think it's appropriate.

For vegging plants that I want to keep happy a little longer in smaller containers, I use Better World insect poop/frass, which stays

Good water is essential if you want to grow gorgeous buds like this one

suspended in the water and is a broad fertilizer rated at 2-2-2 for N-P-K values. I'll use alfalfa meal for this same purpose sometimes for vegging plants for the same reason. Sometimes I will add a small pinch of micronized Azomite with the guano, alfalfa or frass. I will sometimes add just a *tiny* amount of molasses to the water with suspended matter in it, very small, like 1/8th teaspoon of molasses per gallon of water small—don't overdo this or you'll be sorry.

Make Your Watering Easier and Easier

Always be aware of ways to save yourself time and work in the garden. For example, the way I have found to water my plants consistently well and efficiently is using a 2000ml beaker with ml measurements along the side. Since I know how much water each plant's container size needs to be fully watered, I just pour it into the beaker until the desired amount is reached, then just water that plant, and so on. If you need a gallon or two of water per pot, just water once in an empty bucket (using a normal watering can or whatever) that you can measure the water in, and just fill it up to whatever you need and take note how many seconds that took to pour that much water out of the watering can; you savvy? At first switching to the TLO style will seem kind of cumbersome and alien even. That's alright, that's completely normal. You will "organically" evolve into the dynamic and it will get much more simple and easy as you go on and learn—and this happens quickly, too, using this book as a guide.

> **REV'S TIP** Couple last gems here, first, if you want to really kick a tea up a notch, try adding a small frozen cube of bloodworms (frozen fish food) to your tea per gallon; I like to blend these up in a small blender with some water before adding to the bubbling tea. Another really exotic addition to teas I like almost always is bee pollen, and especially for flowering plants. The pollen seems to really bring out all the finer points of smells and flavors in the final product. Most good health food stores will have bee pollen for sale.

HELPFUL TLO TIPS

- Now, these days I no longer use anything like CaMg+ in my water, but, for a long time I did use it and it worked very well. With the new soil recipes in this book you shouldn't need to supplement any calcium or magnesium in your water either, but since there are always a lot of variables from any grow to any other grow, you might. One thing these days that I do add to my water always is some water from my fish tank, just a little bit, 1 or 2 oz per gallon of R/O water. It dawned on me one day that water should be alive, and these small additions from my fish tank water accomplish this, along with bringing my water's PPM up to about 30 or so, which is fine, and all great elemental stuff. I use 1 oz additions for flowering plants and 2 oz additions for vegging plants, due to the high levels of N in the fishy water.

- Adding too much calcium and/or magnesium to your water will actually lock these two elements out, and you will find this is almost always true with any additions or amendments you use; so ratios are very important, and always start out very light with anything new you are trying out.

- When making teas for your baybees, remember to keep all the additions on the lighter side; and, it is super handy to have a little inexpensive TDS meter to help you stay on top of the PPM ratios of your water and your teas. If your plants look great until about 3 weeks before they are finished, and at that time they take a hard ugly dive, then you are likely just putting too much PPMs of stuff on them in flowering and it's building up in the end and biting you in the ass; so back off.

- A pinch of Epsom salts bubbled per gallon of living tea can be a super good thing and sometimes plants of a certain genetic makeup will have an extra powerful "thirst" for magnesium that can be satisfied this way with ease. Just remember that if you use teas a lot then they will need to be of lower PPM value than if you make teas rarely. As a rule of thumb I try and keep any teas down below 80 PPM and I use them less often than most peeps. If you like using them often, then closer to 50 PPM would be a better target. Just dilute teas with pure water to get to the desired PPM level.

CHAPTER 8

Composting and Mulching

Better and Safer Composting

Composting is a huge part of TLO, so this section should be considered very important. Technically, TLO growing is about decomposing organic matter, both mineral and organic, and it is the very same processes that happen in the compost pile and in your growing containers. The microlife decomposes organic matter for food, and they help to decompose mineral elements as well, with enzymes, acids and other exudes. Fungi usually handle the more dense matter, initially, until it is broken down sufficiently for the bacteria to take down further. Wood and some mineral elements are two good examples of these types of more dense things, which fungi prefer to process normally.

The term Hot Composting refers to compost piles at least 3 feet x 3 feet x 3 feet in dimension. Hot compost is packed with a great supply of available nitrogen and is full of organic matter, like guanos and manures. Lawn clippings, alfalfa and blood meal will also get these piles "cooking"; they get very hot on the inside, creating temperatures that manifest a whole different level of bacteria that love some hot organic matter. Temperatures of 150°F are pretty common. It is also essential to turn these larger piles fairly often, so for the sake of sparing myself a ton of work, I just compost in my tumbler. It always gets really warm, but with about 2 extra cups of alfalfa meal it would get nice and hot—still, not 150°F hot in my tumbler, but pretty hot.

The more airflow you can get to a large compost pile the hotter it will get, because more air means the pile can support more life at once. Sound familiar at all? The trick to keeping compost piles non-stinky is to keep them well aerated and turned often—*Boom!*

> **REV'S TIP** TLO is all about composting. Nature is all about composting, and, dare I say the universe is too. I always call composting "cooking" and if you get good at cooking stuff, your plants will seriously blow your mind, I promise.

Bird & bat guanos always need to be composted before use; hot composting fresh guano is always best if possible. When handling dried or fresh bird or bat guano, you should always wear a respirator mask with the kind of filters that are designed to keep fungi spores out of your lungs. Things like dried chicken guano can really cause you huge problems if you inhale it. There are some nasty fungi that like to hang out in dried bird and bat poop in nature/outdoors, so wear your mask anytime you collect it. Please get a good mask, as many of the things you will be mixing, like perlite, can be hard on the lungs without having

A respirator mask is essential when dealing
with certain soil mix additives

anything to do with fungus or toxins; perlite dust is just an irritant. A higher quality mask is a must have, and the slightly higher cost will seem negligible when you realize how dangerous such things can be. In my opinion, the painter/surgical-mask type is not good enough for guanos (fungal spores) but works okay for perlite. Things like these nasty fungal spores that lurk in bird/bat guano are actually uncommon, but, it only takes once; basically whenever there are a ton of floating particles of anything in the air and you have a mask, put it on.

Manures Hot composting kills virtually any "evil" microbial life that may be lurking in barnyard manures; regular slower styles of composting are all good too, and normally just fine, as long as you know the animals who donated the manure are healthy. Still, it's better to be safe than sorry, so always hot compost if possible! The warmer the composting material is, assuming there is enough (enhanced) air flow, the faster it will finish, and the finer of a grade of compost you will get.

Note: Now, it will also finish composting very fast if it contains good stuff and you *never* turn it, it will be HELLA-stinky though, due to the non-air breathing microbeasties (anaerobic) that will colonize it from the inside out. This actually also works fine to make great compost if you don't mind the horrid stench, as I have seen many times, as long as you turn it over regularly for a couple of weeks before you use it to get more of our favorite air breathing microbeasties (aerobic) colonizing the decomposed matter of the pile. This way also gets very, very hot!

Composted and shredded bark mulch isn't pretty, but it is very useful

Like anything else, you'll get good at composting things, and all you have to do is not give up easily when it gets all messy before you dial it in. Making mistakes is a huge part of the learning process; be tenacious and you will prevail. Use the compost tumblers if you can. What a labor saver; well worth the hundred bucks in my opinion; you can make (I do) all TLO soil-mixes in compost tumblers and it works superior to any other method I have ever used.

Shredded bark mulch is a very important part of any living soil mix, period. Avoid anything from a walnut tree here due to walnut tree parts having a crazy pH raising effects in soil, as I understand it. Always try to locate composted bark mulch, preferably shredded, because it will cause there to be less decomposing of that mulch and will therefore preserve some of the nitrogen that would otherwise be temporarily unavailable to the plant. I make it a practice to sprinkle some top layering with available N on top of the soil mix, just before adding the bark mulch. This gives both the plant and the microbial life a rich source of available nitrogen so they won't compete so much for it up top. Also, make sure your bark mulch is in its natural state, with no dyes or paints added for esthetic value.

I use shredded Douglas fir bark as my mulch, but I have used redwood bark, pine bark, even cedar bark, and it always worked just fine.

> **REV'S TIP** Mulching will also make top dressing with small amounts of things like bird or bat guanos very effective, especially when used in a proactive manner—about two weeks before the plant needs something.

In a supernatural TLO container in a warm growing environment, your mulch layer will be just about gone (decomposed) every 30-45 days and will need replacing.

Always mulch your TLO containers!

Mulching TLO Growing Containers

I notice that many people growing organically indoors do not often use a mulch layer on top of their soil mix. You *always* want to use a mulch layer when TLO growing. The mulch layer is all about enhancing and increasing the microlife population in the soil mix to supernatural levels. This provides an environment that is shielded from intense light, and from fans rapidly drying it out up top where surface roots can hang out much closer to the surface. These conditions are great for all the life in the soil mix, including the roots of your plants.

REV'S TIP   Remember that tons of air is always good when composting. That's why I add a lot of perlite to my worm food, and to my soil mix. When I make compost piles outside I always skillfully use enough twigs to keep the air flowing and I turn it often. Microlife (and minilife) are the decomposers, and they need air. More air equals more microlife, and that my friends results in supernatural growing!

Home Earthworm Farms

Now you don't *have* to have any of these cool little earthworm farms, but boy, are they ever awesome! I have one, and I love it. I have had mine for about six or seven years now, and in that time I have learned quite a few things about them. First of all, you'll learn about all natural nutrient sources, such as potato skins and cantaloupe, and what using them can bring to your resulting earthworm castings. At first I just followed the directions that came with the earthworm farm, and then I tweaked a few things out along the way.

You may be wondering why you'll need all the minerals in the worm farm additions table previously in this book. Minerals break down pretty fast when in proximity to high levels of bioactivity from the microbial life. These minerals are ones that are hard to make available all naturally, like phosphorus, potassium, calcium, and many micro and secondary nutrients as well. All those are very important to your plants, especially during flowering, for the LARGE yields.

The calcium from the oyster shells is awesome, and so is the pH buffering. The coconut coir fiber is a fairly effective pH buffer too, and the worms also seem to really love having it around and seem to really

breed prolifically when I use it. When the coir breaks down (which it does pretty quickly in TLO and in worm farms) it brings decent amounts of K into availability in the soil mix. If your earthworm food seems too wet, just add some more shredded junk mail and dry coconut coir to it, and if it is too dry just add some chlorine/chloramine free water or moister kitchen scraps. The real key is to keep it somewhat moist, but never dry or super soggy either.

The humate (humic acid ore shale) really adds to the availability of secondary and micronutrients in the castings. The kelp meal brings in good amounts of K, growth hormones and enzymes that are beneficial, and micronutrients too. The alfalfa brings in great nitrogen, iron, and Triacantanol. Triacantanol

Rev loves his indoor earthworm farm

Leachate tea from an earthworm farm is
really high in totally dissolved minerals

is a growth hormone, and a very special one at that, and as far as I know it is only found in alfalfa. The perlite is an absolute must have; no doubt about it. It enhances the castings' ability to cycle air throughout and so enhances the microlife populating the castings; a win-win situation. I actually got a juicer right after purchasing my worm farm, so I eat healthier now and always have great food scraps for my worms too.

These home worm farms all normally have a spigot at the bottom for collecting leachate worm "tea" from. You have to watch it if you use my recipe here, because that worm tea is super high in TDS/PPM (totally dissolved solids/parts per million) so it must be heavily diluted just before using and only used occasionally. Don't use this stuff for every watering or the excess mineral salts will build up in the root zone of your container plants and you will need to flush them very well in response. I normally just pour any excess leachate tea back in the top tray whenever I add new worm food, or use it diluted on houseplants and in the veggie gardens.

REV'S TIP I now freeze any excess worm juice into cubes in ice cube trays for use whenever I want, and this works fantastically. Freshly collected liquid out of the worm juice collection container works perfectly mixed with water (like a fast tea) in small amounts—like 1 teaspoon per 1 gallon of water small—and not often either; I do this about once per month or so when I have access to the worm juice. Seriously, once per month.

EASY TLO FIXES FOR PEST PROBLEMS

The best fix is always not to have the problems to begin with. However, this is not a perfect world and let's face it, shit happens.

I have looked deeply into many types of controls for pathogenic and parasitic attacks on your cannabis plants, so here's your fast reference for some of the über-important things you need to know whenever you plan on killing things in a living organic garden. These will also make sure you or your friends/patients aren't poisoned.

Bugs and how to get rid of them:

- **Spider Mites:** Safer's End All II, neem oil and liquid castile soap mixtures work well against these suckers. Alternating every third time using the neem x liquid castile soap works well in my experience using End All II the rest of the time. Shield your soil mix with paper plates or saran wrap while dripping. Organocide is another option; however, this stuff is beyond stinky, like dead fish stinky, so not really for use on an in-house garden.

- **Powdery Mildew:** Neem oil x liquid castile soap mixtures work well to remove the mildew from your plants. However, you will need to be "addicted" to using this about every 2 weeks to keep it under control. Many times special tea recipes will work well when applied foliar style (sprayed on to the plant leaves). Get some high quality milk and dilute it to 9:1 water/milk and spray it on the plants (foliar style). This often works very well. Serenade is my old go-to method for fighting powdery mildew; it works very well, but it is also pretty offensive smelling.

- **Thrips:** Treat these like spider mites above. The big difference with thrips is with diligence you can totally eradicate them, while spider mites are much harder (if not impossible) to eradicate utterly with treatments of safe warfare.

Pest fixes that should NEVER be used in TLO:

• **Hot Shots No Pest Strips:** Don't think for a second that these are even kind of alright to hang in your gardens. You may as well be slowly spraying your plants with Raid or Black Flag insecticides. Read the directions on these little poison bombs and you will see they don't recommend it to hang where there are people or pets; now why do you suppose this is? Smoking poisons that kill well is not a good idea.

• **Avid and Floramite:** No friggin way, not once, not ever! Anytime something says it is meant for ornamental only, that is your warning that it is POISONOUS! Don't be a dead dork!

Great choices for TLO pest warfare:

• **Bio Warfare:** There are a lot of natural predators out there available for purchase to combat various pests like spider mites. Most indoor grow rooms run hot and at very low humidity. This is really a fast death sentence to most predators, so really, once again I have to say an ounce of prevention is worth a pound of cure. Spider mites for example just love it hot and uber dry, because they are hooked up to the plant and get all the water they need to avoid dehydration.

CHAPTER 9

Building a TLO Container Mix

Let's Build a TLO Container Together

For this example, let's use a 2-gallon container—the size of container I like to flower plants in—under 400 watt metal halide Eye Blue lamps. My plants rarely get over 3 feet tall when finished under the 400 watt lamps, and this is perfect for me. Building our containers from the bottom up, use a new or clean 2-gallon container; I like to spray the inside of the container with a little water before anything else, and this allows any nutrients applied in a layer on the floor to adhere and start processing faster.

TLO containers in action

This is exactly how I build my containers:

Sprinkle about 2 teaspoons of something dry and high in nitrogen on the floor of the container, such as blood meal, or high-nitrogen bird or bat guano. I actually use my custom high-nitrogen layer blend (also found in this book) for this purpose.

Sprinkle about 1 tablespoon of dry, all-purpose nutrients, like Organicare Pure Grow or Bloom, or something all natural with equal N-P-K numbers as close to the same as possible.

Fill the container with some TLO living soil so your plant will be at the right depth when placed into the new container.

At this point I used to use some granular myco fungi product sprinkled in the container so the new root ball will set right on the myco granules.

Small collection of healthy clones growing TLO style

Good buds require a good TLO container mix.
This beauty is growing under LEDs!

Good myco fungi—granular and soluble versions example

You don't need to worry about any myco anything at this point if you already have inoculated this plant before with myco; they're still alive and thriving as long as you haven't killed them.

Place the root ball down on the soil in the container and fill with either 2-2 Supernatural Soil Mix Recipe 2.2 or Recycling Soil Mix Recipe, and pack soil down around sides GENTLY.

For this first watering, before making the spike holes, use about 1 quart of water and make sure you get the entire surface of the soil wet. Wait a few minutes then make your spike holes close to the outer rim of the container. Remember, you don't want the roots to reach these spikes for at least a couple days. Fill the spike holes with your chosen fill mixes. I of course recommend the custom spike mixes I showed you previously, as they are proven winners.

Time for a little topping off (top layer) with about ½ tablespoon of custom high-nitrogen blend, or high-N bat guano. Sprinkle this around

REV'S TIP As a rule of thumb, the day I am going to build containers, I cut my TLO soil mix with some (living) earthworm castings (and maybe a little more perlite); sometimes I mix it up the day before I will need to use the soil. You certainly don't need to do this; it's just a little tweak I use. This inoculates the whole container mix with a big influx of massive microbial life and diversity—so your mission is not to kill them—plus it will aerate better, which is always a good thing.

Plant flowering for five weeks in my TLO-built containers

The almighty self-watering container   The bone meal move

on top being careful to avoid getting any right up next to the stem.

A layer of shredded, composted bark mulch is added as the final topping. Make sure it's around half an inch deep or so.

Water the soil mix very well, allowing the runoff water to freely drain off. I use an additional quart (at least) of water this time, and allow to thoroughly drain before putting a catch tray under.

Whenever I transplant any plants, I use a pump sprayer or something similar to spray off the leaves and wash and debris or dust off of them. This is a good habit to get into. I call it "raining on your plants" for obvious reasons.

Anytime you think you may have pissed off or killed the myco fungi, re-inoculate using a soluble version like the Great White product I use. Avoid dosing your plants with high-phosphorus liquid organic nutrients, because this will really have a negative affect on those good myco fungi. Never, ever pour ANY liquid fertilizers on plants/soil using the TLO philosophy; you may think it's a good idea at some point, and the results will often look good in the very short term, but you will screw yourself out of the supernatural experience!

The steps above show you exactly how I build 2-gallon containers

> **REV'S TIP** Keep in mind earthworm castings are already cooked (composted) so they're all good to add and roots will love it! Do not add any global raw minerals or things like kelp meal here, as these things should have already been added ahead of time and cooked in for the best results and this is a common mistake new TLO growers will make, adding something like some kelp meal to the soil-mix that has not been cooked yet; this almost always dives your pH low.

This TLO garden has a dedicated room for building container mixes

Compartmentalized and well-organized soil mix stations with various amendments visible

The end product is great container mixes for your plants

Very tidy container mix ingredients

for flowering. I *always* like to put these freshly transplanted females back into their vegetative state for at least a week, before flipping them over to the flowering photoperiod for good. This makes for happier plants that yield bigger, in my experience; and happier plants always make for happier smoke—Amen.

Transplanting into Self-Watering Containers

This procedure is essentially the same as for the normal pots. The first thing you do is spray down the inside of the whole container a little, then you add perlite, or a perlite/vermiculite or perlite/coconut coir layer to fill the bottom section, using enough to just cover up all the lower venting holes. Spray this layer down a bit with a sprayer.

PHOTOS: MONICA GRIFFIN

Additives for the soil mix,
including oyster shells

Container mixes ready for use

Well-organized amendment shelf

This TLO garden has a great
container mix room, with all
ingredients clearly visible

Add a thin layer of soil mix about ½ an inch deep or so on top of the perlite layer, then do the nutrient layering using this thin layer of soil as the "floor" of the container as we did above for the regular pots.

Add another layer of soil mix about an inch or so deep (whatever depth you need) on top of the nutrient layering to place the root ball on to. Fill and then spike (as per above with regular pots) as per usual.

Sometimes for transplanting plants into their flowering containers, I will place a stripe of bone meal in a U shape as shown in the photo. Be very sure the roots have room to avoid the bone meal if they want to, so don't sprinkle bone meal covering the whole lower soil surface. You add the bone meal stripe at the same time and on the same "floor" layer as you added the other nutrient layering elements, and as above just cover with about an inch of soil mix (at least) to place the root ball on top of. This works really well and I do it often.

CONTAINER BREAKDOWN:
2–3 GALLON SIZE

Here is a side view of a typical flowering container size I use for flowering under a 400 watt Eye Blue metal halide HID lamp. I am a bit disabled so the ability of TLO style to flower in these sized containers is a big help to me.

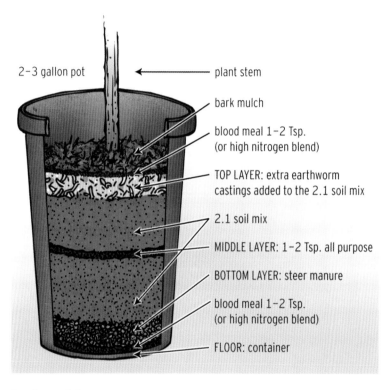

2–3 gallon pot — ⟵ — plant stem

bark mulch

blood meal 1–2 Tsp.
(or high nitrogen blend)

TOP LAYER: extra earthworm
castings added to the 2.1 soil mix

2.1 soil mix

MIDDLE LAYER: 1–2 Tsp. all purpose

BOTTOM LAYER: steer manure

blood meal 1–2 Tsp.
(or high nitrogen blend)

FLOOR: container

Bark Mulch

This is just shredded bark mulch you can get at any nursery and many other places as well. Just make sure it is not painted or treated with anything, and if it is already composted that is always a bonus too.

Blood Meal 1 – 2 Teaspoons

I sprinkle this down on top just before adding the bark mulch layer over it. Avoid getting blood meal or any nutrients too close to the main stem and keep it kind of out more toward the edges of the container. I use the custom TLO high nitrogen blend here, but bat/bird guanos that have high nitrogen work well also.

Top Layer

I like to add extra earthworm castings to the top couple inches of 2.1 soil mix at a ratio of 2 parts soil mix to 1 part extra castings. This really gets things going well in the container, regarding the microlife equalizing.

2.2 Soil Mix

I usually cut this with about 25% earthworm castings the same day I transplant to inoculate the soil mix fully with massive bacteria, fungi, nematodes, amoeba, etc.

Middle Layer

This is where, during the filling with the 2.1 soil mix, I will put down a layer of some quality all-purpose dry organic/all natural nutrients. My favorite is to use about 1 teaspoon of Botanicare's Pure, then sprinkle in about 2 teaspoons of pure worm castings right on top of the all-purpose, then continue filling with the 2.1 soil mix.

Bottom Layer

Here I use the custom TLO steer manure blend and do NOT set the root ball of the plant you are transplanting directly on to this layer; it can go very wrong sometimes. Always have some normal soil mix to place the root ball on to, so don't make your bottom steer manure layer too thick.

Floor/Blood Meal

I use about a tablespoon of blood meal or custom TLO high nitrogen blend here on the floor of the container before anything else is added. You can also use high nitrogen bird or bat guano here as well, and if the variety is a longer flowering type, you can also put about a tablespoon of dry all purpose down on the floor as well along with the high nitrogen elements.

CHAPTER 10

Recycling Your TLO Soil Mix

My compost tumbler baybee

Here we go with the third and final prong of the TLO methodology. First let me say that you really will make this a whole lot easier if you get yourself some kind of compost tumbler(s). They come in a lot of different sizes. But kiddy pools, thick tarps, big totes and rubber animal troughs all work fine to recycle your soil with, as well; it's just a lot more work. If I was doing this on a large scale I would build *large* tumblers that you could spin around by motorized means, or maybe hook up a bicycle to it to spin it. Whatever works!

This practice has come full circle for me, and now I *always* recycle my own mix. When I say full circle, what I mean is that when I first started doing soil mix recycling, it was very simple. At some point thereafter, it became a very complex set of rules and formulas, and it really didn't work as well so I eventually went back to a simpler set of formulas. The soil mix that I use these days has been recycled and re-recycled for six or seven years now and I get stellar results. If it seems complex to you, keep in mind we are aiming at container growth here, which is a very unnatural situation for the plants, so they need a good diversity of additions to grow vigorously within intense indoor growing environments.

The Soil Mix Recycling Container(s)

When I basically toss old root balls (soil and all) into a container to recycle them, I prefer the container to be a tough plastic cooler, but a plastic tote or a plastic kiddie pool will also work fine. I only need one recycling container because my cannabis garden is just my own little

Yields almost as big as hydroponics yields can be harvested using TLO

> **REV'S TIP** To put TLO soil mix recycling into its most basic terms, you are replacing some mineral elements and organic matter that will decompose to a humus state or pre-humus state, where it supplies the plant with very available nutrient values. Microlife and minilife are responsible for breaking down all (almost all) organic matter. Cannabis roots are the main staple here for recycling as prime organic matter FULL of nutrient values, and as luck would have it the roots of cannabis are full of all the same exact stored nutrients that cannabis loves! Imagine that: You are about to become a supernatural grower.

personal one, taking up only a single small bedroom and a couple of additional grow-tents. If your garden(s) are larger, then you might need a couple of containers or more. Essentially recycling is easy: Break up the root balls with a shovel and then add water and they will begin to break down before making your recycled mix. It's that simple. Don't get it too wet, but make sure it is well moistened and always allow air to reach it. Never seal this type of container from air exposure.

Two big advantages when using the cooler are the insulation and the drain plug, the latter of which is fantastic to have if you add too much water. It is very important to either have a drain plug or make one. Too much water will turn anaerobic fast and start to smell really horrible. Anaerobic soil mix kills roots on contact due to things like alcohol that are produced by these anaerobic microbeasties that don't need any air to breathe. Indoors, I use some shower curtains or a good tarp underneath these containers and that has always been great for containing small spills. With time you will get a "sixth sense" about how much water to add, and how often, to keep it just a little moist and not soaking wet. You need a bit of space in a garage or shed to recycle soil mix, but I have recycled with tarps and coolers in a 15 foot x 20 foot x 8 foot bedroom with a small closet, and that was large enough for me to rock it; with plants flowering in that room as well, and the closet full of clones!

I used to add all kinds of stuff to my soil mix as it recycled, like all my leftover cannabis plant matter, stems and leaves, along with things like kelp meal, alfalfa meal, steer manure, greensand and Dolomite lime. Since I got my own little worm farm, they do most of the big work for me, and my recycling mix only actually needs to process the cannabis roots. I highly recommend the worm farm approach to recycling, as it actually makes everything much easier to recycle, and faster too. If you prefer, you could also go down the route of a home com-

RECYCLING SOIL MIX RECIPE

The 3–3.5 cubic feet of recycled matter is your base point here. If you have 7 cubic feet of recycled matter, just double the rest of the recipe. If you have only 1.5 cubic feet of recycled matter, just halve the rest of the recipe. Math is your friend!

- 3–3.5 cubic feet (18–21 gallons of used soil mix/roots/plant matter/kitchen scraps, etc.)
- 1–2 gallons of coconut coir (flushed/rinsed)—optional but highly recommended
- 2 cups powdered Dolomite lime
- 1 cups prilled, also called pelletized (fast-acting), Dolomite lime; use additional $\frac{1}{3}$ cup powdered dolomite if no prilled available
- 1 cup blood meal
- ½ cup bat or bird guano (example 9-3-1 for N-P-K values)
- 1 cup Azomite granular (use $\frac{1}{3}$ cup if powdered Azomite is used)
- 3 cups feather meal
- 3 cups bone meal
- 1.5 cups greensand
- $\frac{1}{3}$ cup powdered Soft Rock Phosphate / OR 1 cup granular Rock Phosphate (try hard to get this, bite the bullet and do it online if need be, highly recommended)
- 2 cups all natural rice: some may sprout, don't sweat it (optional)
- ½ cup humic acid ore granular by Down to Earth brand (optional but highly recommended)
- ¾ cup gypsum powdered (2 cups if granular gypsum is used)
- 3 cups kelp meal (heaping)
- 2 cups alfalfa meal (optional but highly recommended)
- 3 cups crushed oyster shell (OR 1 cup ground oyster shell; A.K.A. "oyster shell flour")
- 4–8 cups of composted steer manure (optional, but always try to use at least a little, and barnyard manure will also work here)

posting unit, like my compost tumbler. It's all about getting a bunch of healthy broken down organic matter back into your soil mix, so whichever way suits you best is the one you should choose.

These days I use totes to hold my recycled soil mix and another tote to hold used root balls for future recycling. For recycling root balls and cooking them to make the Recycling Soil Mix, I exclusively use a

My recycling containers of choice are plastic totes and coolers

compost tumbler with the additions spelled out in this book. I also use a worm farm for kitchen scraps and extraneous cannabis plant matter like leaves and stems. If I didn't have a worm farm I could still just recycle everything in the compost tumbler no worries. Just chop and bust everything up pretty well before adding it to the tumbler and you are golden.

Raw Organic Matter Considerations

When composting, it's very important to understand that raw organic matter tends to burn "hot" at low pH values while processing (cooking) and is *not* root friendly during this process. In nature, organic matter decays mostly up top, slowly working its way down towards the roots (via gravity) as it is broken further and further down. However, in a well-aerated soil mix like a TLO mix, if you have something like alfalfa or kelp meal mixed in the soil uncooked, and you put your plant in there too, things will not go so well. Even Dolomite lime, especially the powdered variety, needs to be cooked into the soil mix just like organic matter does, otherwise lime in a raw reactive state does not get along well with roots or micro/mini life. Any organic meals, blood meal, cotton meal, etc, that are organic will fall into this category and need to be cooked first. All guanos and farmyard-type manures need to cook (compost) before use—always. This is all important stuff, so make sure you "get" this, or else you will end up killing innocent plants—and when you kill them this way, they die ugly!

> **REV'S TIP** As far as kitchen scraps go, you can add anything organic that has spoiled or has not had much butter or salt added. Avoid oils too. You can add some things like fruit pieces and peels, and onions too, along with peppers, but you have to keep these additions at a minimum due to their high levels of acids. Some of my favorite things that rock for nutrients are: cantaloupe rinds, banana peels, potatoes and skins, watermelon rinds, and corn husks and used cobs.

Put it all in the compost tumbler and spin it around five or six times. Make sure it is moist throughout but not soaking wet. If you have living worms riding through the recycling process from them living in the root balls, make sure you place your compost tumbler in direct sunshine for only half a day, max; otherwise, if you have no worms—which is all good too—you can put it in full sunshine and cook it (done in two weeks for sure in full sun). I would almost always cook it for 30 days, just because it's always better if cooked longer than needed. Recycled soil not cooked well enough will cause you big problems.

Note: All the old recipes from the first edition of this book will seamlessly blend into the recycling methodology, and most all of this is based upon empirical knowledge.

If you do not have a worm farm, then you can also recycle everything else within the compost tumbler; stems, extra leaves and kitchen scraps, and whatever else is compost worthy. Just chop everything up well. You can also accomplish this in a kiddy pool or on a tarp or whatever, but it takes longer to cook unless you can turn it over well every other, or every third, day. The compost tumbler really makes primo supernatural recycled soil that is very alive!

I like to mix up about half or ⅓ the amount of soil with all the amendments and simply add that last to the compost tumbler. Several spins of the tumbler will blend it all together quite well, but it will become better and better as you work the tumbler over the next weeks.

> **REV'S TIP** You need to have the compost tumblers outdoors or on a tarp indoors. I find rotating them 180 degrees every other day works best while cooking, but you can just turn it over a couple times a week, if you need to visit it less often.

EASY FIXES FOR NUTRIENT PROBLEMS

When you are TLO growing in containers with my suggested recipes and formulas to start out with, you cannot experience a nutrient deficiency. However, if you do have a problem nutrient, use this guide to troubleshoot your issue.

- **Potassium deficiency (K).** This often has to do with your environment being too hot and dry which raises your plants metabolism and they almost literally sweat out the potassium. Molasses, kelp meal, greensand, and alfalfa all bring in good levels of potassium, and make sure to add enough greensand when first making your soil mix as a proactive measure that works awesome.

- **Nitrogen deficiency (N).** Nitrogen is easy to supplement with liquid fish fertilizer in teas. Top dressing with high N bat or bird guanos will work within 10 days or so. Feather meal in your mix is actually very important here as a proactive measure, because in a supernaturally alive soil mix even blood meal can be consumed über-fast. Feather meal has staying power and is especially important when building containers for longer flowering sativas.

- **Phosphorus deficiency (P).** Never ever pour liquid phosphorus rich fertilizers on; this will completely screw up the myco fungi in the container. Spikes, along with additions of Big Bloom liquid in teas, you can keep the fungi happy and healthy while still enriching the soil mix. Cannabis can store enough P to take her about half way through flowering (4 weeks).

- **Sulfur deficiency (S).** This looks a bit like an iron deficiency. Gypsum and soft rock phosphate are both great proactive ways to avoid this from being deficient in recycled soil mixes. Running ambient temperatures too high during lights out time can interfere with sulfur uptake and absorption. Foliar feeding with dissolved Epsom salts will work in an emergency and allow about a week to take effect, spraying every day.

- **Magnesium deficiency (Mg).** Greensand, soft rock and rock phosphate all bring in some Mg, and molasses is usually high in Mg too; around 8%. Molasses and or CaMg+ should fix a lack of this up used mellow but steady, in about a week..

- **Calcium deficiency (Ca).** Ca and K are closely entwined in TLO growing, and when you have an issue with one, the other will almost certainly show up. Too much calcium is normally the problem here, and you should be careful of your water source and any calcium liquid additions you use. Oyster shell, bone and feather meal, dolomite lime and gypsum, and the liquid CaMg+ I use at 10 drops per gallon of pure water are all good for calcium and cannabis. Avoid hard water, or using too much liquid calcium.

- **Manganese overdose (Mn).** The problem with manganese is it is usually in fluctuation as far as levels go in ground water. City tap and well water will sometimes be very high in manganese at certain times of the season depending on rainfall amounts. If your pH dives for any reason and there are high levels of manganese present too, you can get a fast and deadly result in your garden. Always best to start with pure water I think, for so many reasons. Mn is present in mineral additions and I have never seen it deficient.

Recycling Soil Mix Important Note

The Recycling Soil Mix Formula in this chapter is designed ONLY for pure (nominal PPM, like below 10) water sources while also recycling a wide diversity of organic matter, including a fair amount of acidic things like coffee grounds and even some fruit scraps, and it will even make super indica plants very happy by just adding water to this soil mix—no extra nutrients needed—however, if you are forced to use a water source with PPM up around 60 then cut the dolomite lime and oyster shell additions by a third. If you are using a harder water source like spring or well water that is up above 150 PPM, then cut the dolomite lime and oyster shell additions by two thirds and the bone meal by one third. These are guidelines for you to use, however I recommend using pure water sources.

CHAPTER 11

Teas

Impressive seeing living container worms

My teas and my whole tea philosophy and methodology have undergone some serious evolution since the first edition of my book. Tea recipes in the first TLO book were excellent as long as you were able to have your containers running maximum populations of microlife at a high metabolism. I see those old recipes as a bit too complex, and I have now made them much simpler. Big changes include the regularity of my use of teas. These days I give my plants two or three teas max during their entire flowering period. If you are not using spikes, you will need to use them about once every 10 days or so. Another change is I have made them mellower now, and again, those complex recipes are no more.

Teas are like *accelerated* highly aerated liquid cooking factories that cook the organic matter they contain, and even minerals they contain to a degree, due to all the bio-activity in the proximity of these mineral elements. You'll love two major aspects of the true Supernatural TLO Living Tea the most:

Using all the same all natural additives in your teas as in your soil mix spawns microbial life that's dialed in to take faster and better advantage of those exact same elements. Always use your teas within 24-30 hours after the tea was made and started bubbling. This is the time of maximum microbial populations and good foam on top is always a great sign. These times can vary a bit due to ambient "brewing" temps.

Always scrape down the sides of any container you use to make tea. Use a rubber spatula well below the liquid tea's surface level, and mix this sludge back into the tea before using. Remember to stir the tea between use so all the particles you scraped from the sides get distributed evenly from plant to plant, as these most awesome particles tend to sink, and within 30 seconds a good deal of it has hit the bottom.

Add a little bee pollen to your teas when your plants are about two weeks away from entering their flowering photoperiod. I use around ½ teaspoon per gallon of "brewing" and bubbling tea. Since I dilute my teas by about 80-100% with good water just before using them, this would equal out to be ¼ teaspoon per gallon of finished tea. Go to a health food-type store and see if you can get small amounts of fresh bee pollen; refrigerated versions would be my first choice here. See what you think.

What Is A TLO Tea?

TLO teas are technically types of organic compost (or vermicompost) teas, also known as AACT (actively aerated compost teas). The term "vermicompost" is used to describe the sort of compost you get from using earthworms, as the final product will contain composted matter as well as vermicast, otherwise known as worm castings, otherwise known as worm poop. Since I have my own earthworm farm I always use fresh vermicompost as my AACT inoculant (with some fish tank water very often as well). You see, my green friends, healthy compost and/or earthworm castings are just teeming with life: huge populations of bacteria, fungi, protozoa, nematodes. A "tea" is just some earthworm castings or compost rich with microbial life that is then bubbled in an organic solution of mostly water and some nutrients such as molasses

One-half gallon of actively aerated compost (vermicompost) tea

and dried fish meal, which are added to promote a population explosion in the bubbling organic tea! The bubbling process can be achieved by using a cheap air pump, some air tubing, and an airstone in smaller tea bubblers.

Connect the air stones to some air tubing and
place in the bottom of the tea container!

If you use compost instead of worm castings to inoculate your teas,
make sure it is *healthy* compost. Bagged compost and earthworm castings are often all fine and good. Just make sure they haven't been sterilized, and if you see any living worms in the castings, then you can
assume with high confidence that it will be great for your purposes. You
could easily just use a little of your own TLO soil mix to inoculate your
teas; life is everywhere! Once again, adhering to TLO philosophy here,
we are inoculating our teas with the same source elements in our soil
for maximum efficiency.

The actual nutrient power of your teas for your plants comes from
two basic elements of the tea after it has been "brewed" for about
24-36 hours. First, from all the crazy huge populations of microlife;
many of the amendments added to your tea have been processed
into very tiny (humus and almost humus sized) particles, and these
small particles are very easy for the plant roots to absorb. Secondly,
from the life itself present in the tea. All these tea-born microbeasties
are packed full of great nutrients as well and these nutrients are temporarily immobilized (unavailable to the plant) until the microguys die
and are processed themselves. Bonus!

REV'S TIP   The Sandstone type of airstones just keep on
working and I have been running the same one
now for a year at least; it's still going strong!

Sandstone airstones
work primo

You can make your teas bubble
using air stones like these

Using your teas within the 24-36 hour window is a good thing so the massive life still living in the tea can enter your containers and continue processing nutrients from the soil mix that will in turn feed the plant. So letting a tea brew for days—or past when it is foaming, around 36 hours from the start—still results in a nutrient rich solution of humus and near humus particles. You just don't get that extra kick with the sudden influx of the same (massive) numbers of microbial life. The film that will stick to the sides of your brewing container needs to be scraped down and blended into the tea, as this is a treasure chest of humus sized particles, and these scrapings are über-microlife-heavy.

Note Regarding Large Scale Garden Teas

Let's say you are brewing very large batches of teas for your plants, in 55-gallon plastic cans. You don't need to use 55 times the amount of dry and liquid additives.

That's right. Not only that, but you don't need to spend your money on any kind of commercial tea brewing device. You only need a decent air pump and a few airstones to keep it bubbling well. Just make sure the inside sides are smooth to allow you to scrape them down after brewing.

Using our 55-gallon example, assuming we will add good water after brewing to make it around 100 gallons of tea, you would initially add say ½ a cup of bird or bat guano and like 1 cup of kelp meal. You can experiment with ratios to dial it in yourself; this is just to give you an idea of those ratios. As far as something like molasses goes, for this example, I would use about ½ cup. It's easy to tell if you use too much because your tea will either not foam, or barely foam, after the initial 24 hours of brewing.

Teas should foam up after several (like 12) hours. If they foam up immediately, this is not a sign of massive life present, but actually a sign that there are fish emulsion, and/or yucca products present. Teas that spawn massive life tend to foam up after about 8–12 hours in a room where the ambient temps are in the mid 70s (F). I use teas about twice or three times during their whole flowering period (plants that flower 8–10 weeks) and double that for longer flowering 16-week varieties.

For all the following tea recipes, always use chlorine/chloramine-free, high-quality water, and for my little personal garden I bubble my teas in a 1-gallon pitcher, but I always dilute the final teas 80-100% using good water, doubling the tea's liquid volume before use. With all the following teas I will give ratios for bubbling/aerating 1 gallon, which ends up as 2

Opaque customized Rev tea bubbler—light shielded

gallons of tea just before usage in my gardens. Since I have a smaller personal garden, and I use a perpetual flowering dynamic, I don't ever need more than a couple of gallons of tea at any one time. If you use the standard grow and harvest dynamic with all your flowering plants at the same stage of maturity you can just up the size of your tea brewing container to however much you will need, and read above regarding big tea brews.

If you do not add CaMg+ to all your garden water like I do, and you use pure water like rain/distilled or R/O water, you will either need to add CaMg+ to your water for the teas (15 drops per gallon of brewing tea) or cut your water by about 20% with bottled spring water. You just need your tea water to be buffered with some dissolved minerals to enhance the bacteria populations. Don't even *concern* yourself with the pH of your tea—have a little faith.

Ultraviolet light (UV) really hurts the microlife in your teas, so always keep that in mind; just like roots and earthworms, they detest light, and in the case of the microbes, it kills many of them. Sunlight is the worst, and direct sunlight will really make your tea weak in life compared to even shaded sunlight. HID grow lights are pretty bad too, especially the "Blue" types that I like to use. Ambient temperatures when making teas should also be around those that are comfortable to people; 70–80°F is perfect I think. You can see in the picture that my tea bubbler is shaded. I painted the pitcher with flat black paint then reflective silver, all-latex-based paints.

REV'S TIP If you are brewing your teas in very warm temperatures they will finish faster than the 24-hour period, and in cooler temps they will take a little longer.

STANDARD TEA FOR VEGGING PLANT

This is a basic tea recipe I use on vegging plants when I need to keep them happier for a longer time in smaller containers, or if I want some rapid growth to happen in short order. Again, these ratios are to brew 1 gallon of tea, which will be diluted into 2 gallons before use. The truth nowadays is that I rarely use teas on my vegging plants, simply because the TLO Supernatural soil mix has plenty of nutrients to supply vegging plants, even big ones in fairly small containers. For the guano in this recipe make sure the P value is no more than 1/3 of the N value, and the P value should not exceed 5.

This tea is great to use during vegging all the way up until about 10 days before they will go into flowering. Do not use on seedlings or freshly rooted clones.

- 1 teaspoon kelp meal
- 1/4 teaspoon dry soluble kelp/seaweed
- 1 teaspoon alfalfa meal
- 1/2 teaspoon of high-N bat/bird guano (example 9-3-1 N-P-K values)
- 1/2 teaspoon feather meal
- 1/4 teaspoon blood meal
- 1/2 - 3/4 tablespoon molasses (max)
- 1/4 teaspoon all-purpose dry grow fertilizer (example, Organicare's Pure Grow)
- 1/8 teaspoon Azomite powdered (micronized if possible)
- 1/2 teaspoon ground oyster shell
- 1/4 cup earthworm castings (or compost, or 2 teaspoons of worm leachate juice)
- 1 tablespoon insect frass/guano (optional)
- 1 teaspoon Humes Gardening Blend, kelp/humus/yucca (optional)

You will see some serious growth over the two weeks after using this tea. I wouldn't use this tea more often than once per 10 days.

> **REV'S TIP** The biggest problem I see people having with teas is they start treating them like nutrient solutions and overdose the plants with them either too often or using more additives (or higher ratios) than necessary. You know that one of the fastest ways to screw up a fish aquarium is to be adding too much food? The same rule applies here. Teas are like nutrient solutions to some degree, but they are also so much more. Try out my suggested ratios before deciding to modify them and I think you will see the true TLO power of the teas.

I then used that little red plastic plate as the lid. Always set your tea bubblers on some type of plate or tray to catch spillover liquids from the teas foaming over the top, as this almost always happens when your teas are rocking well. I still—at the time of writing—use this same tea bubbling shielded pitcher.

FLOWERING TEA

For use from two weeks before flowering starts, until the halfway through flowering.

- $3/4$ tablespoon (max) all natural molasses
- 1 teaspoon alfalfa meal
- 2 tablespoons of Fox Farm's Big Bloom liquid (optional)
- 1 teaspoon Humes Gardening Blend (optional but highly recommended)
- 1 teaspoon insect frass/guano (optional)
- $1/2$ teaspoon bee pollen (optional)
- $1/8$ teaspoon Azomite powder (optional but highly recommended)
- 1 teaspoon kelp meal
- $1/2$ teaspoon dry soluble kelp/seaweed
- 1 teaspoon feather meal
- $1/2$ teaspoon dry all natural bloom fertilizer (example Organicare's Pure Bloom)
- $1/2$ teaspoon balanced high-N bat/bird guano (example 12-8-2 for N-P-K values)
- $1/4$ teaspoon high-P bat/bird guano (example 0-10-0 for N-P-K values)
- $1/2$ teaspoon fish meal or dried fish (example 11-5-1 for N-P-K values)
- $1/4$ cup earthworm castings (or compost, or 1 teaspoon of worm leachate juice)

Also I would like to point out here that if you have your own earthworm farm, your leachate worm tea is a fantastic inoculant for the AACT TLO teas you are bubbling. The leachate contains vast populations of a wide variety of microbial life. If you feed your worms like I do, your leachate tea will be über-high in PPM with dissolved minerals, so just a teaspoon or two of leachate in a whole gallon of bubbling tea is enough to inoculate it with booming life waiting to happen!

FINISHING TEA

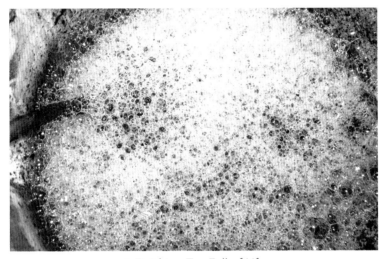

A Finishing Tea Full of Life

This finishing tea is used from halfway through flowering until 2 weeks before harvest.

- 1 teaspoon kelp meal
- ¼ teaspoon high-P bat/bird guano (example 0-10-0) OR, bone meal as a sub
- ½ tablespoon (max) molasses
- ⅛ teaspoon Azomite powder
- ¼ teaspoon bee pollen (optional)
- ½ teaspoon Humes gardening blend (optional)
- ¼ teaspoon dry bloom fertilizer (Organicare's Pure Bloom for example)
- ¼ cup earthworm castings (or compost, or ½ teaspoon of worm leachate juice)

> **REV'S TIP**   You sure don't need to suspend any bags of organic matter in your tea solution; that's more how a regular cup of drinking tea would be made. I have found it far better to just let all the matter be freely added to the solution to be stirred by the bubbles. If there's any sludge left in the bottom of your tea brewer after use, don't waste this. Either add it to your recycling/cooking soil or use it as a top dressing on some garden veggies, houseplants or trees.

The following recipes are made in 1-gallon containers, for diluting with an additional gallon of water before use. All water should be as pure as possible and chlorine/chloramine-free with the addition of CaMg+ or spring water as in the vegging tea above.

Make sure the guano used in this recipe above has *at least* half the P value of the N value.

If you really feel the need, you can strain your teas when you pour them out of the tea bubbler. I no longer bother with this, because it's an extra step that is—in my experience—unnecessary. All the heavier (larger) pieces of the tea additions will settle to the bottom of the tea brewer rapidly, so it's really no big deal.

Make sure the high-P guano has no N value at all to insure the high-

Better World insect guano (Frass)

TLO tea brewing equipment

Note the well-organized tubing with easy access valves

DIY tea brewing equipment working away

est resin production from your plants flowers when they are finished. There's enough available N in this finishing tea to supply the microbeasties with the N they need while not having enough for the plant to access in any amounts that would hinder resin production.

Some Special Tea Additives Examined Closer

Humes Gardening Blend is a dry custom blend of soluble humate, kelp and yucca, combining the attributes of these three elements into a synergistic soluble powder. Humes Organic Gardening Blend helps improve soil's ability to retain, process and release moisture and nutrients, making them more available to plants when they need them, and is a source of naturally occurring plant hormones and nutrients.

Insect frass is essentially dry insect poop and insect pieces and is a great source of things like chitin, calcium and many other great nutrients and normally runs about a 2-2-2 for N-P-K values. I use Better World brand for my insect frass source.

Bee pollen is a nice addition in very small amounts. Although there is no specific chemical composition, as this varies bee colony to bee colony, the average composition is said to be 40-60% simple sugars

Custom soil mixes and teas are the way

(fructose and glucose), 2-60% proteins, 3% minerals and vitamins, 1-32% fatty acids and 5% diverse other components. A recent study of bee pollen samples showed that they may contain 188 kinds of fungi and 29 kinds of bacteria. Despite this microbial diversity, stored pollen (also called bee bread) is a preservation environment similar to honey, and it contains consistently low microbial biomass. While I find honey to *not* be a good addition to my flowering teas, I really like the bee pollen and it really seems to kick the tea into high gear as long as it is used sparingly, like a very powerful spice would be used when cooking food.

> **REV'S TIP** If you just follow my lead and use two or three teas total for your flowering plants I think you will see how well this works. I use a tea at the two weeks before entering flowering point (vegging tea) and another about two to three weeks into flowering (flowering tea) and another about three weeks from harvest (finishing tea)—boom! It's as simple as that my green amigos. All these wonderful teas will slowly add these special elements to your overall soil mix making it even more diverse and full of life.

Freshwater from aquariums is primo as an inoculant, as long as your fish tank hasn't had any bullshit used in it like stuff for removing chlorine, sick fish treatments, etc. You can use this in any tea and I use it at a ratio of about 1oz per gallon of bubbling tea.

Soluble and liquid kelp and seaweed are very powerful tools. However, this is also very often a grower's problem when this is used too often, or when overdosed even once. The overdose issues usually show up as a K problem or salty issue as well, in my experience. If you use the liquid, be very careful of additives to that product that lengthen shelf life and I would highly recommend you get the soluble dry version as this needs no preservatives. Humes makes a fantastic soluble seaweed product.

Liquid fish emulsion/fertilizers used to be a main staple for my teas but no more. The huge problem here is, you guessed it, PRESERVATIVES like sulfur and phosphoric acids in high ratios. These are not good for your living soil. Use the dried fish or fish meal in your teas. The P value in these dry products is in the fish bones in a bonded state, and is much slower to become available than phosphoric acid added directly to the product for shelf life, and chelation.

If your supernatural or recycled soil mix is TLO style, and you are using layering and spikes in your flowering containers, you won't need any teas at all, unless you are flowering *large* plants in super small containers (I don't recommend this). However, teas will really bring up the power of your flower. As I said, I use two (three if you count the tea two weeks before flowering begins) teas during the plants' entire flowering period. Every TLO environment will be a little different at least, so dialing in your regularity of tea applications will be a fairly simple matter; be observant, and as a big rule of thumb never use teas more often than 10 days apart.

TLO LIVING TEA FAQ

There are tea recipes out there meant for more of a soup style organics grow that work fine for soup style; but a tea that is meant not to disturb the microbeasties too much is a TLO living tea. Here are several common questions I will try to answer as clear as I can.

Q: Would adding greensand to my teas work well for iron, and K?
A: I have never found greensand to be particularly effective in living teas. Your mileage may vary, so try some out with greensand, and some without greensand. Use it on a couple clones from the same plant, and see what you think; I have had many peeps tell me it works great for them and that greensand is uber slow and steady in your TLO living soil. Sometimes I get a wild hair and add some.

Q: If my tea doesn't foam does that mean something is wrong?
A: Not necessarily, it could just be that it is very warm where you brew it and it peaks with foam in like 6 or 7 hours when you are sound asleep, and by 12 hours time the foam has gone again. Or too cool where you brew, and it doesn't peak (foam) for like 18 hours. The only two other big reasons that come to mind are just plain old too much damn food in your tea, or certain high P things like high P bird/bat guano, and soft rock phosphate; you can use both of these in your teas but you must think in uber tiny amounts; just a bit too much of either of these and you will have no foam tea. Yeah, myself, I like using any tea when it is in foam mode the best.

Q: Making my first tea ever, what's your advice for simplicity?
A: Per 2 gallons of distilled/rain or R/O (reverse osmosis) water, use about ½ cup of earthworm castings that are alive, or ¼ heaping cup of composted bagged steer manure. Use some dehydrated kelp/seaweed soluble powder, like 1 teaspoon. Also 2 teaspoons of molasses and something with some fast available N like alfalfa meal, or dried fish, or 1 teaspoon of a liquid 5-1-1 N-P-K fish fertilizer. Bubble it above 65°F and it takes about 12 hours; unless you are very warm. Keep it out of harsh direct intense lighting, if possible; also, stir tea mixture between every plant application.

Q: What kind of PPM am I looking for when using teas?
A: This question is a bit like asking me how often you should water, and because of mucho variables, I would say start lower, and work

Flo by DJ Short TLO-grown and photographed by SnowHigh

your way up. I will say that at different times I have hit my plants with some heavy PPM teas up around 250-300 and higher even. My norm for teas is probably around 70-90 PPM, and I don't use teas often. If you use my soil mix correctly you can certainly just add water and get good results. Teas are more enhancers than they are fertilizers, and you should always think of them this way, you will be foamy and happy—less is more truly applies here.

CHAPTER 12

Troubleshooting

Now, every grower likes to tell you that they have no problems with aphids, spider mites, powdery mildew, grey mold (Bud Rot) or humidity in their grow room. This just isn't true for the greater part; all growers find themselves stumbling over one problem or another from time to time, no matter how fantastic they are at what they do. With that in mind, I advise all of you to read this troubleshooting section well. This is the section in which I will cram a ton of preventative measures that will save you time, money, and frustrations. First, we are going to discuss some pH meters. I recommend you get a decent soil testing pH meter. It doesn't have to be a top of the line type, but it shouldn't be the cheapo version either. For troubleshooting, often times a soil testing pH meter is your best friend, because if your soil mix gets way out of range for some reason, like soil mix not cooked well enough, and you learn that from your meter, then you can fix it by letting it cook longer. If you don't have a meter, you have to play a guessing game that often makes things even worse.

Pruning Your Plants The TLO Way

Let me begin by saying that your plants will use up (drain) all the nutrients and water from larger lower leaves whenever they feel like it, or feel they need to for some reason. In the second half of flowering, your plant may (quite normally) start "draining" her lower leaves of nutrients and eventually water too. The yellowing of the leaves gradually occurs from the bottom up in (the later) flowering stage. Using

Pruning plants to match their environment

the TLO philosophy we treat all the plants' leaves like batteries for the plant to use later. Here some quick points, then we will dive in a bit deeper, because I think this is very important for quality, and especially for higher yields.

Don't remove leaves until they are all used up

I only ever prune my plants at the same time I transplant them. I feel this keeps the plants in the lowest amount of stress, given that both the transplant and the pruning are stressful things for a plant and even though you are doubling up on the stress sources, the happiness factor for the plant right after gets her through it fast and easy. Since I like to grow indoors, and I favor grow tents, I tend to always trim my plants by removing the lowest axial branches; maybe two, maybe eight, depending on the morphology and growth stage. I like circulation down low for the plants, so I tend to keep them clear of any axial branches until at least eight inches above the soil level. If they are topped going into flowering containers, I would want four or six axial branches left on the plant—this can vary a bit depending upon plant morphology, but I have done very well using eight main axial branches left to flower, *many* times.

Never remove any leaves that just look a bit bad, or slightly yellowed; once they are fully "drained" they can be easily broken off from the stem. The plant will use (drain) a decent amount of its leaves before it's done, so let her set the pace, and only remove leaves during flowering once it is obviously done draining them. Using the TLO methodology, your plants can finish with a lot of green leaves left or may use up some of its last (larger) green leaves, right before it's done. This is your window to work within, regarding your usage of spikes, teas and layering.

Never waste the drained leaves. You can safely lay them down on top of the mulch layer to decompose slowly—just chop/crush/tear them up first. However, if I were growing using synthetics, where I have no real soil microbial life going on—at least not really plant friendly ones so much—I would *NOT* place my drained leaves on top of the soil or medium.

Drained leaves as mulch

Drained leaves as mulch after a week

The pruning bottom line is this: Keep some good space between the top of the soil and the lowest axial branches of the plant. This is for several reasons like better circulation down low. For flowering plants you actually get better yields by keeping a topped plant pruned down to four to six main branches when transplanting into the flowering container. Under a 1000 watt bulb/light I would alter that to six to eight axial main branches. Keep in mind, to yield larger (than untopped) overall from a topped plant, you will need to supply greater resources for that plant, like container size being larger for starters.

Fungus gnats can bug you but a couple are all good. In a TLO garden, this will likely be an encounter you will have, because life wants to happen there, and while these little flying buggers can really annoy

Pruning is an ongoing process and all leaves are recycled in a TLO garden

you, both they and their larvae fill a niche in the TLO garden and are, believe it or not, beneficial in several ways that I know of. The good news is that I have a fix for you; the only "bad" news is it takes two weeks to work, and they drop off almost totally at the two-week mark in my experience. Please call bullshit on all the bad hype about these gnats and look into it for yourselves. If I were using synthetic nutrients, I would be *very* concerned about a gnat infestation, because they actually do (seem to) damage to synthetically grown plants; with no food (living soil) around the gnat larvae seem to go after the plants' living root hairs.

The Safer Garden Dust is essentially dormant BT (*bacillus thuringiensis*) bacteria that are normally used by organic gardeners and farmers in order to infect caterpillars that do significant damage to plants, killing the larvae (caterpillars) naturally. This works by the caterpillars actually consuming the BT powder dusted on the leaves; great trick and it works awesome. **Note:** Outdoors you need to be really careful using this product, say if you are near an endangered species of moth or butterfly.

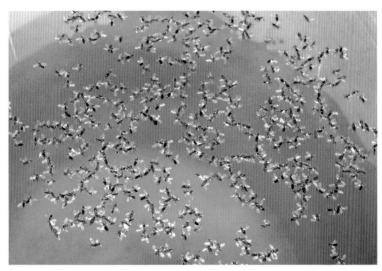

Fungus gnat invasions, oh my!

I had someone tell me once to just use BT in my soil to fight the fungus gnats, and I remember he said that he too had living earthworms in his all natural indoor garden, and the worms were unaffected by the BT in the soil. Now here's how I used it, and after I used it, as I kind of suspected, it took two weeks, almost to the day, and boom! My gnats were gone! The fungus gnats, while not moths, have a larval stage like moths do. The BT for sure seems to be able to adapt to these gnat larvae and kills them just like the caterpillar larvae stage of the moths.

Safer Garden Dust with BT

Inoculating your soil with Safer Garden Dust with BT is a very simple thing indeed, and it doesn't take much (per plant) either, about a $\frac{1}{8}$ of a teaspoon per plant, in any sized pot. Remember, we are inoculating, *we are planting the seeds of new life in the environment,* so just put a little stripe or two down right on top of the mulch layer, away from the base of the main stem, and spray them with a little good water from a pump or hand sprayer just to "scoot" them down into some darkness under the mulch. That's it, and two weeks later it should work the exact same way for you.

Fungus gnat prevention is pretty basic, and I have learned the things they like and those they don't. I can speak highly and personally for the above method. Any kind of barnyard manure will attract them in force, in my experience. I have also seen them get pretty thick using good amounts of blood meal up top under the mulch. They also seem to have a desire for shrimp meal, which is like a catalyst if used along with a high N source like manure or blood meal. They aren't as happy with bird/bat guanos up top.

Sometimes they will come on a little bit strong in some numbers and if they do, those hanging sticky flypaper things you unroll work really well for any minor outbreak, but eventually, recycling and using the TLO philosophy and methodology, you will experience an actual invasion, so bite the bullet for two weeks and use this method. Hang up a ton of fresh sticky traps during these two weeks and you can take a good bite out of them yourself if they are super thick. You can read all over the place how fungus gnats are diseased and yada yada; all I have to say is in a TLO garden, they are made from the same exact stuff as your plants and all the soil life (and you and I). They only carry disease if they have come into contact with those pathogens, which is not bloody likely in a supernatural TLO garden. I like to see a few of them flying around, because their larvae aerate soil, process organic matter and transport bacteria all over the place. So let's cut them a little slack on the bad reputation, eh?

Soil Testing pH Meters

I like my meter with a longer probe so that I can test pH at deeper levels, and this one has a 12-inch probe—big enough for anyone! This comes in pretty handy especially if you recycle soil, because once the raw organic matter has been broken down (cooked well) in the recycled mix the pH value will raise. If I am in a hurry to use some soil mix that is still cooking, I will check the pH and once it gets up above 6.2 I feel it is fine to use it, *unless* I am growing Hashplant type Indica plants, which prefer pH ranges

above 6.5. I have had a few great growers tell me about how worthless soil testing pH meters are, and now that I have had mine for several years, I think I understand their opinions—though I do not agree. Measuring soil *accurately* using a pH meter requires some skill, both to use and maintain properly. Never ever use steel wool on a pH meter; always use those plastic scrub pads and clean paper towels. You must

The Rev uses a Control Wizard soil pH testing meter

TLO grown running perfect pH

> **REV'S TIP** Since things like earthworm castings, compost, and manures can vary widely in their nutrient values, when recycling your soil TLO style you may need to add more of certain things, such as gypsum (for sulfur) and greensand (for iron and potassium). So it's fairly important to identify any deficiency yourself. Since we all don't have access to a lab to test our soil, do it the old fashioned way, judging by the health of your plants like I do.

thoroughly clean and wipe down the meter probe before and after using, every time.

If checking a container with a plant in it, make sure you know vaguely where your spikes are at, because they will run different pH ranges than the rest of your soil mix. Always make several checks in a row, reading each one, and this will really help you see the true reading zone of your mix. I keep my meter in its package so it is not just hanging out in the air, as it does react very slowly with regular air over time. I recommend keeping it in some kind of sealed container or freezer bag for these very reasons. Also, never use any kind of cleaning fluid, or alcohol on the probe; only water if necessary.

To tell you the truth, if things are set up right in TLO growing, you really have zero need to concern yourself with pH meters of any kind.

My very favorite Hanna liquid pH testing meter

However, while you are learning to grow TLO style, or even just organically in a soil mix, I highly recommend you get yourself a halfway decent soil pH-testing meter. It will really help you to narrow down many kinds of problems immediately, rather than months of trial and error testing for what is wrong. Please, rather than getting a cheap soil pH meter, don't bother getting one at all; the cheap ones all suck in my experience.

For Liquid pH Testers Hanna Brand Rules

As long as you are not mixing up mad organic liquid fertilizer blends, you probably will only rarely (if ever) have any need for a liquid pH-testing meter. Again, as above with the soil meter, these are nice to have if you can afford one. Hanna brand meters are the only brand I will ever get (for testing the pH of liquids) if at all possible. They are bulletproof, and they stay calibrated for the greater part over *long* time spans. Don't worry about a liquid pH meter if you are going to grow the TLO way, you really won't need it. I mostly use mine these days to troubleshoot other people's garden troubles.

These are handy for reading/checking new water sources out, or giving you an idea of how liquid additions affect the pH of your teas. Many people new to TLO growing will inadvertently use a liquid organic fertilizer that is full of organic acids added for chelating nutrient elements and to lengthen shelf-life. These types of all natural/organic liquid nutrients can really take pH levels down far, which will adversely affect microlife, in my experience. If you can afford it, a liquid pH meter will save you time and money by having it, it's handy sometimes.

Note: I would *always* go with Hanna brand for a liquid pH meter.

Totally Dissolved Solids/Salts (TDS) Meters

TDS meters used to be pretty expensive but lately they have come way down in price and you can get a fine one for $30, no worries. These meters read in PPM (Parts Per Million) and can give you a relative idea of the levels of dissolved minerals (salts/solids) in a given water source. So say if your tap or well water reads 300 PPM on your TDS meter, then that is some über-hard water that's full of dissolved calcium, magnesium, and other (?) elements. You would find it impossible to grow TLO-style in containers indoors with water that high in salts. However, if your tap or well water was more like 60 PPM then you would have much better chances of that water working alright in your containers indoors, assuming, the dissolved elements were in balance and not high in Mg, Fe, or sulfur, which is common

I use mine to check things now and then. For example, I would use it in my organic teas to measure amounts of certain liquids I add sometimes such as CaMg+ by General Organics, which is a mineral supplement. I will add this to my tea-making water before adding anything else and I will add it until my TDS meter reads 70-90 PPM, which is about 15 drops per gallon. My reverse osmosis water is less than 10 PPM just out of the filter, and that is great for TLO growing in containers. I will check my pure filtered water too from time to time to make sure my reverse osmosis membrane is still working well. I recommend you get one of these if you can, because they are very handy and inexpensive.

Note: Please do not concern yourselves with the runoff water from your TLO containers regarding PPM/TDS values; it's high, don't worry, be happy—you need to lose that synthetic thinking thang—*wink*.

Recycling Soil Mixes With High Ratios Of Peat Moss

High ratios of peat moss in a bagged soil mix often work well for cannabis growing, and I have certainly used plenty of them in the past with good success. When you are planning to recycle your soil mix, though, you should probably reconsider these high-peat mixes and avoid them. I have noticed that, for some reason that escapes me, the pH just wants to drop when you recycle this type of soil mix. I theorize that it gives the fungi a bit too much help somehow and they tend to dominate the container soil mix, and of course whenever they take over like that they love to drop the pH way down low. After having this problem persist and mess up a few plants I decided just to avoid using anything with any big ratios of peat moss in it and the problem was solved.

Here's the new good news; as long as you recycle extraneous cannabis plant matter and kitchen scraps and roots I am pretty sure the high peat ratio soils in bags won't pose such a threat. However I would still keep my eye on it if for some reason I had to use a bagged soil mix of this type (high in peat moss); I would go the extra mile here and use good solid bagged organic soil mix for making your Supernatural Soil Mix Recipe 2.2 if at all possible.

Over Compaction and Anaerobic Problems

In containers, it is especially important that you understand the whole compaction dynamic. Using a living soil mix as we do in TLO growing, it is imperative that you grasp the whole concept of organic matter breaking down, in other words decomposing, or cooking, as I like to call it. Something like coconut coir fiber added to your soil mix will indeed help to aerate it at first; and then, in the highly bioactive TLO soil mix, it begins to break down rapidly into smaller and smaller particles, on its way to becoming humus, and compacting more and more the whole time. Anaerobic conditions can set in and living roots will die if this happens. Plants will die an ugly death. Using something like bark mulch in the bottom of your containers for aeration will do the same thing, and this mulch will likely become anaerobic fairly quickly in a living TLO soil mix. Use perlite, my very green friends. That is your prime aeration amendment in TLO container growing and your rule of thumb if winging it is to use about 20-25% perlite; so if I had 4 gallons of TLO soil mix, about 1 gallon of it should always be small, nugget-sized perlite.

If you lift your growing containers to check their weight when judging how dry they are, always be careful to set them back down *gently*. Repeated dropping of your pots even a short distance will really compact your soil in your containers quickly, like within a month or less. There are exceptions, like heavy ratios of perlite, and large root systems in smaller pots, but in practice it's good to get into the habit of setting your containers down *gently*.

Soil Not Cooked Long Enough

This relates to the heading above somewhat, because often times anaerobic conditions will prevail in containers that are using TLO soil mixes that are undercooked (not composted fully yet). Your plants will get very ugly, stunted and could easily be killed by making this mistake of rushing it a bit to fast to use your TLO soil—let it cook! Don't worry; on the flipside of the coin, you can let it sit after it is done for a very long time; the nutrients don't evaporate, so don't worry, be happy, and over cooked is a good thing!

Lighting Sources, Lighting Habits and Bulb Life

Sure, you can run the whole grow and flowering using fluorescents, even compact fluorescents, but you will be disappointed by comparison to using a real growing light. I recommend the Eye Blue MH bulbs for full term vegging and flowering. TLO gardens just don't do as awesome under HPS lamps in my experience. With the indoor garden lighting industry just exploding, by the time you read this book there may already be some type of superior lighting available, but for now, my recommendation is still (2016) go for the Eye Blue MH bulbs. If you are going to use HID lighting, go the extra mile and get the Eye Blue Halide bulbs. They are well worth it in my opinion and experience. You always prefer a fuller spectrum from any lighting you use TLO growing—*duh*—because the

REV'S TIP   There are some LED lights by Bysen at the time of writing that are leaning towards a fuller spectrum, and I am fairly excited to see these lights myself, as I have high hopes for them. I am also testing out new Plasma lighting at the time of this writing, by Chameleon brand. So stay tuned to SKUNK Magazine for these results as I have them.

plant can use that (sunlight-like) spectrum to help process all the nutrients naturally. Lights down around the 3000K range are not only lacking in spectrum bandwidth, they are abnormal and unnatural to the max.

Please use timers, and I highly recommend digital timers if you have the wherewithal to program them correctly—in other words, don't be really baked while programming digital timers for your gardens. This way, even with power outages, all your equipment stays right on schedule thanks to the battery backup in these timers. These are super easy to find for 400 watt lamps and are also easily affordable. While you are at it, get *true* surge protectors for your lights and it will keep them operating at full potential for a longer time. Not just a power-strip, a SURGE PROTECTOR! Be wary of the tiny little LED lights on many power strips and surge protectors; they should be blacked out with electrical tape or otherwise not allowed to shine their lights during the dark cycles of any flowering plants, or else hermaphrodites could easily be the result. I also find that the Eye Blue MH bulbs work fine with a surge protector between the timer and the (digital) ballast; sometimes Eye Blue bulbs and digital ballasts don't work every time they are supposed to. This is an easy fix and a good surge protector will cost you like $25 (USD).

I run MH bulbs for 1 year on a flowering photoperiod before I replace them. HPS bulbs can go 1.5 years in my experience before needing to be replaced. Make sure to use some type of record keeping about the date on which you first fired up your bulb. I use a simple piece of masking tape on the hood with the date marked using a Sharpie. Also computer programs like Outlook have calendar programs with reminders, and your phone usually has a scheduling application (calendar or reminder apps) for reminders. You can always go with the most reliable and just mark it on a larger type calendar in the grow room itself.

Lights Too Close To Plant Tops

Keep 400 watt bulbs about 18 inches to 2 feet from plant tops and keep 1000 watt bulbs at least 2' away. This is important, as it will cause the very top of your flowers to go into enhanced metabolic activity, and the plant won't be able to mobilize enough nutrients and water faster than the hyper metabolic state causes them to use those elements. With halide bulbs this will normally show up first as a potassium issue; using HPS lamps too close to flowering tops will often case the plants to bolt at the top, making many little "fingers" or calyx towers as I call them (A.K.A. "foxtails). The calyx towers are a normal genetic expression in many old world kick ass sativas, so don't confuse the two. The first sign that your bulbs may be too close is crispy leaf blade tips, and while this is harmless to the plant, it is a little heads up for you that the metabo-

Over watered youngster

lism is jamming due to light distance and/or ambient hot temps and low humidity.

TLO growing works better with your lights backed off a bit from what you would run them at using something like hydroponics with CO_2 additions to the air. Too much heat is a very bad thing during late flowering *especially*, and temperatures at the plant tops when lights are too close are often 10°F (or more) higher than the growing room temperatures. 86°F is the hottest I let the tops of my plants get for any sustained period of time, and I consider 83-85°F just about perfect. Sometimes solving an issue is as simple as increasing the distance between your light source and the plant tops.

Over And Under Watering —The Most Common Error In TLO

I still make this error from time to time, you know; shit happens. This is no big deal if it happens once in a while, but when it happens a couple or a few times over the course of a couple of weeks you will start to

Over watered youngster after proper watering for five days

see problems happen that are often mistaken for nutrient deficiencies. The amount of water any plant uses over the course of a day, or a week or whatever, is very easily gauged by you with little effort and just a couple of brain cells.

Measure your water and get a grip on approximately how much water it takes to thoroughly water any container size; for example, in my self-watering 11-inch (2-gallon) pots it takes about 1600ml (about 1.5 quarts) to thoroughly water a plant that wants and needs water. My 3-inch square pots need two full draws on my turkey baster to fully water. In normal containers, using catch trays, the perfect amount is however much is needed so that whatever water ends up in the catch tray under the container is sucked back up within 30-40 minutes after watering, and the pot is nice and heavy afterwards.

Under watering once in awhile is no biggie, but as above with over watering, if this happens too often your plants will start to hurt; have a guideline of around 1.5 quarts of water to fully water a 2-gallon pot, and adjust accordingly. How warm and dry/humid your growing environment is, will of course play into how often you will fully water; so will plant size relative to container size. If using the self-watering containers, in a pinch you can just make a fast watering job out of filling the bottom trays just using the little lip opening at the base of the containers to fill from. Sometimes if I am going to be gone for a day or two I will water all my plants, wait about 30 min after watering them, and top off their bottom tray by filling it up. The design of these containers is awesome and this is no worries for the roots in these self watering pots.

> **REV'S TIP** There is a pretty simple way to proactively counter over watering, should that become a thing you have a hard time not doing. Simply up your perlite ratios by about 10% or so. To prevent under watering use self-watering containers and put your watering times on a schedule you can stick to. When plants are in containers they get very stressed over a lack of water, much more so than outdoor plants in the ground.

Power Outages Countermeasures

So, your plants are in flowering, your lights are on, and boom, the power goes out! No worries, all you need to do is supply some kind of light, just enough so you can see. This is as much as the plants will need to fool them into thinking it's still "daytime" and even candles work here, but I prefer the little LED lanterns best, and they last a long time. You could pull this off for a few days and you would still be good with no problems from the event, just stay on your photoperiod schedules. Be very, very careful please with candles; be smart, and have a fire extinguisher handy in your grow room(s).

The downside to that is that you have to be there in order for this to work. Alternately, if you are at work all week and can't be there, I have a solution for you, but you MUST NOT ever forget the schedule for this solution. You just plug a couple of those rechargeable "safety flashlights" that stay plugged into the wall socket and automatically come on if the power fails, a couple in a 10 foot x 10 foot room is plenty. The real trick here is that you have to remember to plug them in whenever the lights come on, and UNPLUG them just before the lights go out. You cannot fuck up here, because one mistake and you are boned if the power fails even for a couple seconds during their dark cycle and you forgot to unplug them. If your plants are deep into their dark cycle and the power goes out and those safety lights pop on, you will get hermaphrodites almost certainly 6 -14 days later. This will really screw up an otherwise primo sensi harvest.

Under watered youngster

Grow Room Temperatures and Venting

This is a big deal! This is one of those classic things that will come back and bite you in the ass around flowering time if you do not address it in the beginning. Generally speaking, between 60–86°F is a good range of temperatures between "daytime" highs and "nighttime" lows, but somewhat colder is still fine at night, and the temps in my room go from about 85°F with the lights on, and about 60°F with the lights off. Once again I want to reiterate: Beware of the temps *at the plant tops* during times of higher temperatures! This can cause big trouble and unless you check it, you won't know for sure. Be proactive here; please just take my advice and check it. Portable A/C units can really help with hot temps in your grow room, but they need venting out, and they use a lot of watts and amps.

It is hard to overdo your venting, and fresh air is key. I don't like to supplement CO_2 when growing TLO, but if I had trouble bringing in fresh air I would consider VERY lightly amending the air with CO_2 from a tank, using a timed, intermittent release regulator valve; or I would generate some CO_2 naturally. If you are ever messing with CO_2 additions always pick yourself up a CO_2 detector—like a smoke detector— so you don't pull some ultimate stoned move and kill yourself. When you read things like "air exchange" and "fresh air" or "exhaust fans" in growing books, don't dismiss them because this is a huge keystone piece of your TLO grow if you want it to be supernatural, and I have a feeling you do. Always pull your air through rather than pushing it from any inline fan whenever possible. This makes such a huge difference you will be blown away (if you'll pardon the pun). Any halfway decent grow shops will have nice venting fans for sale, and I like Dayton and Elicent brands for reliable fans. I have never seen either one of these brands fail after many years of use; and the Elicent fans are also super quiet when operating.

Cannabis is pretty well equipped to handle some high temperatures, even in containers if there is water, but it is not that good at handling temps when it gets too cold, and she will have troubles absorbing potassium and phosphorus if the room temperature gets much below 55°F and you will start to see the telltale signs of absorption problems, with purple striping up the stems from the lack of potassium (K) being absorbed. Everything is still all right at this point, but it is a flag for you to see that your temperatures may need to come up a bit during lights off.

When running hot gardens, have your environment be warming up to its highest temperatures for at least three hours. Try to not let the garden exceed six or seven hours of temps above 86-90°F (at the plant tops). The garden temps should decrease slowly over the last two or three hours, before lights go out as well if possible. This is optimal for super happy fast growing plants. I'm just saying, I do it—so you *know* there's a reason, right? Try it, you'll like it.

Nutrient Deficiencies and Starvation

If you are following my recipes, you won't have any nutrient deficiencies, period. With so many plants being grown and bred using synthetic (force fed) nutrients, many kinds of genetic qualities are mostly "unknown" because the whole dynamic of synthetic growing is to force feed a ton of nutrients, which then only allows the roots to absorb a very small percentage of those nutrients. The rest must be flushed away or it will cause lockouts. Growing all naturally using TLO, you get to *actually see* which plants (or strains/genotypes) more efficiently absorb, store and use the nutrients available to them. Some plants are hogs for things like potassium and nitrogen for example, while some may have a hard time absorbing or metabolizing these, or other nutrients, when compared to other strains or individual plants. If you are a breeder, why on earth would you *not* want to be able to observe and know these things? Also, if you kill or fully piss off your myco fungi with high-phosphorus liquid flowering nutrients, your plants will likely begin showing signs of deficiencies of P and K (and often N too) and will force you back on to the liquid nutrients to finish them. Now this can be done all organic, but the final results will be a step below what is possible using TLO—see for yourself before you rush to judge this.

Usually, deficiency symptoms are all too often a sign of nutrients actually being locked out, from pH-related developments you inadvertently caused somehow. These mistakes include using too much molasses or kelp/seaweed amendments, using hard (high PPM) well or city water with a high pH, or using a pure water source with liquid organic nutrients that are full of chelating organic acids can also do it. If you went very simple style, say you didn't use spikes and you were flowering a fairly large plant in a smaller pot, then it could actually be starvation from lack of any available food; best fix if you are sure of this being the case is a nice tea and a top dressing—wait 6 – 10 days and boom, your plant should show some new joy.

The ONLY liquid nutrient you would ever use would be Big Bloom, ONLY in teas, and not much of it. Besides that, we do not ever use liquid nutrients in TLO in teas or otherwise. Now I know this sounds completely ridiculous to some of you now, but it is the correct path, one big reason being that in nature there are no liquid nutrients. The microlife handle all the feeding, and handle it they do, you just have to let them do their jobs. When I say NO liquid fertilizers, there are other exceptions like the CaMg+, which is a liquid mineral additive, and molasses.

REV'S TIP Surprisingly you can starve TLO container plants fairly easily by underestimating how much the microlife need in terms of nutrients and resources. Remember you truly are feeding the soil mix, because it is alive, literally. Nitrogen and calcium, along with oxygen, are all required very heavily by the microbeasties. One of the reasons I like the Organicare Pure dry granular fertilizer is that it also has added 6% calcium.

Synthetics galore

Synthetic Death in an Organic Environment

This seems to be one of the hardest things for many to wrap their heads around, because if you don't understand the dynamics, it seems fine to add a little synthetic nutrient. That couldn't be more wrong, my green friends. If you pollute your soil mix with ANY synthetic nutrients, that soil mix will no longer be able to support supernatural levels of microlife, due to the hyper-dehydrating qualities of those synthetic salts. As soon as your soil begins to dry out a bit the salts hyper dehydrate the microbial life. So avoid using anything with synthetic EDTA or anything like it, ever, on your TLO soil mix. It's almost impossible to flush these synthetic EDTA types of salts out of soil.

If you do make the mistake of using some synthetics on your container plants, the only way I know of to recover healthy plants to harvest is to either stay on the synthetics for the duration—yuk—or, switch over to some kind of heavily chelated organic nutrient like Earth Juice that uses large amounts of organic acids to make nutrients absorbable for the duration.

Avoid being fooled if trying out new products. There are a ton of tricks they use to fool the ignorant and make them think they are using organic methods, when in reality, they are not. Read all labels very carefully.

Here's a partial list of a few things that are NOT good for TLO growing:

• **Fox Farm:** Tiger Bloom, Grow Big, Marine Cuisine and American Pride all have synthetics in them.

• **Botanicare:** Any of their liquid products have synthetic salts, with the exception of the Organicare division of theirs, which does have a large selection of organic liquid nutrients that are heavily chelated with organic acids like Earth Juice products.

• **Earth Juice:** While these products are usually all natural, they are also normally full of organic acids for chelation, and will really dive your pH and piss off a lot of your microlife, especially the myco fungi, it seems to me.

• **Superthrive** is wicked bad, as it contains serious chelating elements and will seriously fry your TLO plants.

Mycorrhizal Fungus Concerns

Plenty of you reading this who are thinking that you are all organic and are using the mycorrhizal fungus religiously are wasting your money. Here's why: Anytime you pour a liquid flowering fertilizer that has any real amount of available phosphorus (P) in it, onto your plants, you mess with your myco fungi in a negative way. This causes them to stop doing what they do best, and that is bringing the plants lots of lovely P and other minerals too. It's like the myco atrophy or something; just like your own muscles would atrophy without use. Through many years I dialed in my myco fungi effectiveness, and I am at the point now where I can actually see when the myco "bite" the roots and take hold.

The whole trick here is not killing the myco fungi once they are established, or pissing them off to the point where they go dormant—in other words we don't want our myco fungi rendered useless. Global available P (liquid) is the enemy here, my green friends.

Since I only inoculate my plants a single time during their life with myco (at the beginning of their life) I use very little Great White myco powder; recently, I noticed some of my sprouts not looking as happy as I am used to and after checking everything, I saw my Great White was like 4 years old! I got some new Great White, and the happiness was restored! So watch for this as well.

I found out the hard way to not use any kind of barley product or extracts. These have a very

This is a carbon filter cartridge replacement

Mighty myco fungi makes big flowers

noticeable negative effect on all the good fungi including the all-powerful myco! I later read that homeowners who have water features on their properties, like ponds and whatnot, often use little bundles of barley to fight algae and fungi build up. Last but not least by any means, DO NOT USE CHLORINATED WATER! As well as chlorine there is a new compound called chloramine and it doesn't just bubble out, so you NEED to filter this out with activated carbon filtering. Chlorinated water just has no place in TLO growing, and I don't ever drink it either these days.

REV'S TIP The first half of the flowering cycle is commonly where many people will over water their container plants. Living soil mixes can hold a lot of water if they are operating like they are supposed to. Anytime I transplant, I like to water thoroughly but then I let the plant go until I see just a little drought stress, before watering again. Drought stress starts to show in the lowest largest leaves first, and they will sag just a tad for a whole day before the rest of the plant will go limp. Over watering can easily cause air to be scarce in the soil mix, so microlife populations diminish, and nitrogen locks out or turns to gas if the problem goes anaerobic. Learn to watch for those bottom leaves drooping, because this is when to water container cannabis, and small skills like this make giant differences.

Salt Related Issues Build Up Over Time

Too much of any kind of salts can really make your TLO learning experience a living hell. Salt problems usually kill plants, but not quickly, rather slowly and ugly. We will go through all the directions I know of that this can come at you from, but always be aware of this, because sea salt and sodium are both OMRI rated, and needed by plants, but are not really good for container plants in any real amounts over time. All salt-related issues look fairly similar and affect the tips and edges of the leaves. The first and most common place this comes from is your water source, and if you have any real amounts of dissolved minerals (salts) in your water—like in city tap, or well/spring water—this can build up in the root zone of your container plants. This will have at least two bad results that I know of: first the salts will tend to dehydrate the root zone for water when the container dries out a bit, and second, those built-up salts will change the pH locally in the root zone, effectively locking out absorption of secondary and micronutrients

Salty cannabis issues in TLO containers

first. Of course the best way to avoid this issue is to use pure water, like reverse osmosis filtered, rain, or distilled water. The other way is a counter-measure: you must flush the hell out of your containers about every other week to leach those built-up salts out of the containers. Even this won't work too well if your levels of dissolved salts in your water are above 150 PPM or so.

Coconut coir fiber is one of the sneaky ways (by sneaky, I mean you won't see the problems arise for a month or longer after you start using it) unwanted levels of salts can build up in your TLO container gardens, and this one will really put a damper on your yields and growth rates too. Sea salts and high potassium salts are notorious in brick coir coconut fiber. Botanicare has an already expanded version

REV'S TIP The synthetic salts used to chelate nutrients in synthetic fertilizers (like the dreaded EDTA) are especially deadly, even in very small amounts in a TLO container, due to the fact they hyper-dehydrate the microlife as the soil mix starts to dry out. Nothing is more anti-TLO than killing off your microbeasties! Don't use synthetic crap, ever, on your TLO containers. Those synthetic salts stay around, and can't be flushed from soil (or plants) so they keep on killing in the soil, and smoking nasty.

of coconut fiber they call "Cocogro" that is well rinsed and works great for TLO container gardens; actually this is what I use in my worm farm *and* soil mixes. Optionally, you can expand and flush the hell out of your brick coconut fiber before use, but you really need to flush it through well, and several times.

Cocogro well-rinsed coconut viber for TLO

Softened water is the last deadly thing on my list of salty offenders in TLO gardens. Softened water sucks for container or any other kind of gardening if you ask me. It is always way, *way* too salty! Now softened water is awesome if you normally have *very hard* water and you hook up a reverse osmosis (R/O) filter to your softened water source, because this will make your R/O membrane last a really long time compared to if you had your R/O filter hooked straight up to a really hard water source. But *never* use softened water on your plants! Just make sure the water softening unit is inline BEFORE the R/O filtering unit and this will actually make your R/O membrane last much longer.

Low Humidity and High Temperature Gardens

If your gardens run up in the very high 80s (F) or hotter, and your humidity is often below 45% your cannabis plants can go through a ton of potassium (K), and I think they actually "sweat it out." If you have really good air circulation in your garden, as you should, this can just exacerbate this specific problem. Now many indoor gardens have to run low humidity because they are infected with powdery mildew, but if you are not infected, then feel free to toss a humidifier in your gardens to maintain around a 50–60% humidity level, like the humidity levels my gardens run at, and this will really help you with accelerated K usage. Otherwise, just keep your K in mind always, and know that things like kelp and seaweed stuff, as well as molasses, greensand, and good, all-purpose dry fertilizer with a good K number are all good ways to make sure the K keeps flowing in your soil/garden. When I used to see this K issue in my grows in the olden days when I had powdery mildew and ran my humidity down around 30% I would just use soluble seaweed in my teas, and sometimes even when I just watered. Again, as with anything, don't go insane with using seaweed extract or you will cause yourself problems with things locking out, like nitrogen!

If you are plagued with powdery mildew, you can bring in a dehumidifier and run your humidity down between 35-45%. This will help slow down the mold a lot. Running a low humidity will also cause your plants (and microbeasties) to go through a lot of calcium, and your plants will also use a lot of potassium in low humidity environments – especially with good air movement. Keep in mind that plants can only absorb calcium and potassium slowly and steadily, so if your air is too hot and dry, you will normally experience a potassium deficiency. This in turn will almost always become a calcium issue as well.

Nuking Your Plants With Nutrients

This can happen with organic liquid nutrients easily, as well as dry nutrients if you apply them too heavily, and/or if you do not cook raw organic nutrients first into your soil mix. If you suspect you have done this with liquid nutrients, flush the container thoroughly as fast as you can, and cross your fingers. If you have done this with dry nutrients then it is almost always game over for those plants. Always cook any dry organic nutrients first into your soil mix before exposing living roots to that soil mix. This overdosing can also happen with normal TLO levels

Nuked plant

Anyone can have problems from time to time

of cooked dry nutrients in your soil-mix, and it will be brought about because you added some kind of liquid nutrient or "enhancer" and changed the pH of the soil mix rapidly. This in turn will cause some of the previously bonded up nutrient elements to start reacting with each other and become suddenly way too available—*not* good!

If you run a worm farm using my amendments be very careful not to get too heavy with your worm casting ratios in your soil mix. These castings are very rich in nutrients, and especially minerals (salts) so just stay with my recommended ratios and you will be all good.

Questions To Ask Yourself

Anytime you make a significant change to your TLO grow, do it one thing at a time, and give it a month or two to see the short, and longer term results. With multiple big changes, you are just FUBAR (*fucked up beyond all recognition*) as far as troubleshooting goes should your changes not work out well. If the plants get bad *fast*, think what happened about two weeks ago, and if they slowly progress with an issue, then think up to two months ago as far as what you did (or didn't) do. Things like tents can stretch over time a bit. If they are vented they contract when closed and expand when open, and over time some of the venting covers' Velcro seals won't be doing their job and a little duct tape is all that is needed. Duct tape also can stretch and peel off over time so any taped up light leaks should be checked occasionally. Any time you find hermaphrodites in your gardens, try to assume it is definitely your fault and not the genetics, unless you are obviously working with questionable genetics. Take some time and find the light leaks or the hard stressors that are causing them. I rarely ever see a hermie these days but 90% of the time when I do, it's always my fault!

REV'S TIP Some of the most devastating mistakes can happen if you are using an un-calibrated or cheapo meter, and it is telling you something very wrong and you are acting based on that information. Do yourself a huge (proactive) favor and if you are going to use meters, make sure they are good quality meters and check their calibration on a schedule.

If you are stumped and there is a problem with most or all of your plants and you just can't figure out what the hell is wrong; ask yourself these (that could apply) following questions:

• When was the last time I changed the carbon filters on my water filter?
• How old is my R/O membrane, and have I checked my filtered water's PPM lately?
• How old are my light bulbs?
• Is there a problem with my venting fan, exhaust or ducting?
• Have I been slacking off on perlite additions to my recycled soil lately?
• Have I checked any potential light leaks like Velcro vent covers with tents, or tape on windows, or light seals on doors?
• Have I started using new ratios, or products (or new sources) lately, like in the last couple of months?
• Have I checked my timers' settings lately, or recently reset them?
• How confident am I in my meters' calibrations/readings?
• How old is my myco fungi product?
• Have the genetics I am growing been bred using synthetic nutrients?

A very happy and healthy female cannabis plant in flower

Photo Reference Guide to Common Plant Issues

You can see in the photos of the perfectly happy cannabis plants how their leaves have great turgor and they are perfectly green and "happy" as I call this look. You will see these kinds of plants a lot once you get going if you follow my methodology. The following is a photo guide to help you identify problems you may be having. I caused many of these problems in my gardens intentionally, in order to be able to show you with photos. Let's start with spider mites, shall we:

A perfectly happy and healthy vegging cannabis plant

Spider Mites

I want to put this problem front and center for two reasons, the first being that this is a very common issue for many of you. Secondly, if you look closely at your plants at least every few days or so (closely I say) and you see what is shown in the photo on the upper leaf surfaces, *this is the time to take action*, right upon sight. In the photo is an example of an early infestation, and within 30 days there will be spider mite webs and thousands of these buggers on your plant. I still say Safer's End All II is your best countermeasure in TLO and the safest I have found. Another one that might work well and seems to be fairly safe is Azamax

Here's what spider mite damage looks like on the leaf upper surface

Here's a photo of mites about to happen
big–soon–needs spot treatment now

(NOT Avid). I have never used this product personally but have heard good things and I have looked into how it kills and it seems acceptable if you have to go with a spray. Catch it early and you can keep them somewhat under control. Read and follow all directions on these types of products, please.

REV'S TIP For Powdery Mildew (PM) issues, I highly recommend the product Serenade; however, Serenade is very foul smelling and should not be used at all during the last two weeks before harvest. The same rules apply to Neem Oil products. The best way to combat PM and spider mites, or any other parasites, is just start over from seeds after having zero plants in your garden for 10 days while your garden is kept warm. (See The Nuclear Option in Chapter 2).

Cuttings Going Badly

This is a common mistake and one you will likely make while dialing in your cloning dynamic. The trick is to not to have too much (close) light, and temperatures that are not too hot (or too cold). Simply raise your light up 6 inches or so if you see your healthy cuttings looking like this before they are rooted enough to transplant. You may opt for

Rooting cuttings and light distance

a lower wattage light too. Temperatures must be mild/comfortable when rooting, as hot temps will increase the cutting's metabolism to a state where it will run out of all its stored food trying to grow before it can make good roots. So again, there is a Goldilocks Zone here like with everything else in the universe. Just dial it in and you're golden.

On the flipside of the coin, cold environments are also a bummer for rooting cuttings and I have combated this in the past very effectively by purchasing a high end aquarium heater and dialing it to keep the cloner water above 68°F and then placing it in the cloner reservoir; it works beautiful! Never dial in this type of heater to above 72°F due to microlife concerns.

Classic phosphorus drop off expression

Phosphorous Problems

In your TLO soil mix you will not ever (or very rarely) need to add more phosphorous (P); the soil is all good and balanced with plenty of everything that the plants need. The photo shows phosphorus drop off just before it is about to get bad. Early signs will be purple petioles at the top of your plant—these petioles should be green up top—and this can happen if you decide to add some liquid P or are using too many high P top dressings. Soil not cooked well enough can do this too. Very cold nighttime temperatures down around 46°F can also cause problems with the plants' ability to absorb P as well. Salts/minerals building up too much from bad coir or high PPM water can also do this.

Worm farm juice overdose with salty results

Worm Farm Juice Overdose

This is what you will see on the lower leaves and mid leaves first, and it will get worse from here. This is one of those times a good old fashioned flushing, using distilled, rain or R/O water will probably help out decently. You must be VERY CAREFUL with the leachate worm juice you collect from your worm farm if you run your worm food using my additions. A very little bit of worm juice goes a long way and the PPM of this "juice" is wicked high with great stuff, but too much of anything is bad. So use this magic elixir lightly and *never* use it more often than 10 days apart.

Root Damage

This often happens after a rough transplant, and in the photo you can see how the upper leaf edges are toasting away and curling upwards, along with a not happy plant overall. The plant in the photo fully recovered in about 10 days, and during that time I just made sure she had good water at proper times and a good low stress environment. Do nothing, that's my recommendation; don't go adding B vitamins or whatever. Just don't do it; you will throw your living soil out of balance and this will not help the plant. All you need is good water to fix this problem, and a little time.

Root damage

Flowering Plants Short on Their Water Requirements

Earlier in this book I showed you a photo of an under watered vegging plant. In this picture you can see how this expresses looks on a flowering plant, at the bottom. Now there is no need to fear here, the plant is simply draining her least efficient leaves of their water and food; it's what adaptive plants do. Just up your watering schedule a bit—not a

Under watered plants look like this down low

lot—and this will stop. But again, it's not a big issue and if the plant has a lot of lower leaves I actually encourage this to happen about halfway through flowering and I pull off all the dead leaves allowing greater air circulation down low. Recycle all these dead leaves!

Simple Nitrogen "Flags"

A "flag" is not a problem, it is just a visual queue for you that informs you of a possible problem in the future. In the photo of nitrogen (N) starting to run low, don't worry, a little top dressing with some high N bat or bird guano (example 9-3-1 for N-P-K values) will make her all good again starting about seven to 10 days from the top dressing. Please don't goose your plant (soil mix) with any kind of liquid N fertilizer fix; this is always a bad idea. This yellowing from the bottom up will continue slowly until the guano takes effect, or a transplant will also fix this flag that your N is just beginning to run low-ish. If you plan to transplant a plant like this within the next couple of weeks, don't worry about it, and moving the plant a bit farther from lights will also

Nitrogen is just starting to run low

Normal nitrogen stuff. Do not panic!

keep her happier with the N she has for a longer time and the yellowing will slow.

As you can see in the photo of the flowering plant with the yellowing lower leaf, this plant is taking N from its lower, less efficient leaves. Nitrogen is mobile in the plant and she can move it around fairly easily to supply more critical plant areas like the flowering tops in the greatest light. Plants do this quite normally, and if it happens too fast it can also be due to over watering. Let her use her stored resources and she will continue to do this more as she gets deeper and deeper into flowering. Plants that flower in a robust manner will start to drain their larger less efficient leaves for water and food earlier into the flowering process. This is what they do, so there is no problem that needs fixing.

Finally regarding N issues, please remember that the microbeasties need a lot of N to work with. In my soil recipes, spikes, layers, and in my teas there is what may seem to you to be unnecessarily high ratios of N. This is not the case, I assure you.

Ca issues–very early warning signs

Calcium (Ca) Problems

This can happen from several causes, and is normally due to a salty/mineral buildup in the rhizosphere of the plant roots. Using excessively high ratios of excellent worm castings (like the ones you would make yourself with my worm food additions) or too much worm juice (leachate) can also bring this on. Too much Ca or K in your soil mix can also have this effect, and don't worry, both the Supernatural Soil Mix Recipe 2.2 and the Recycling Mix already will have plenty of Ca so there is never (except slowly, via water source for example) any need to add more Ca, you savvy?

If you do not water twice, or water thoroughly, you can also see this problem arise. As the roots grow in the pot they start to guide the water flow downwards, along "guided paths" missing large areas of soil mix within the containers; and with insufficient water (per watering) dry spots in the container mix can occur, and this becomes a "dead zone" in the container, very often affecting Ca uptake for the entire plant. Water your plant once (thoroughly) when it's dry, and measure the water it takes so you have an idea what those container sizes require, that's all. Then just adapt your watering skills to ensure that the plants get a good watering when it gets watered. Nobody's perfect here, so just keep your eye on the target. Your watering skills are a prime (keystone) facet of TLO growing methodology.

Proper Ca levels are maintained also through a good wet/dry cycle, and it is always a good idea to let your plants get pretty dry between waterings; just don't let them get to the point of showing drought stress during flowering—drought stress is when the entire plant just goes limp.

Flowering Cannabis Plants and Magnesium (Mg) Issues

In the photo you can see some Mg problems. Buds will be all good in this case, except for yield. Yields in this plant were down almost 20% and while it was very high quality, I hate to miss out on the flowering power of TLO done right. Molasses over usage is your number one suspect here. This can also happen if you have added liquid nutrients that are abnormally high in organic acids, throwing off your whole living

Magnesium issues

soil dynamic. The overuse of KMag (dry element) can have this effect, along with a rapidly progressing N deficiency/lockout. Over watering (and/or not enough container aeration) almost always has this effect on flowering plants as well. There's really no coming out of a magnesium problem that has progressed to the point of the photo, however, if it is due to over watering, this can be partially corrected in about 10 days with proper watering skills.

Don't use liquid nutrients and watch your molasses usage, and all will be well with a good watering habit—always think about watering and how you can do it smarter and better.

Synthetic Death Sentence

You can see the evidence of root damage in the photo of the synthetic effects when used on a living TLO soil mix. Using liquid synthetics or dry synthetics always turns out the same. Your soil life dies, and extreme levels of synthetic salt deposits are left in the soil and the rhizosphere. This will start "choking out" the finer roots effectively killing

Synthetic nutrient effects on TLO soil

them off, and the plant will attempt to grow larger water root morphology to resist this; but it will lose that fight, and the salts continue to build up with every usage. So just don't do synthetics, they suck, in every way, and synthetics are all about corporate greed and death to your living soil—*no thank you!* Never, ever, recycle soil mix that has been exposed to any synthetic fertilizers. You cannot simply flush out salts like EDTA and other synthetic compounds.

Potassium issues

Potassium (K)

In the photo you can see fairly developed K problems, but even at this point the plant can recover if you have used a liquid kelp or seaweed concentrate that is too powerful (too powerful as judged by the microbeasties not by you) or too often, or if you have top dressed with some kind of powerful K salts like KMag. She'll be fine once you transplant and stop doing whatever you did along these lines. Using KMag in your TLO soil mix can cause this too, and I feel the product is better left out, but if it works well in your dynamic, to each their own. Sustained high temps at low humidity—like 40% and below—can really drain your plants for some potassium fast, so think about lowering temps 5°F or so; make small moves, *always*.

Purple stem striping

See the purple striping on the cannabis main stem in the photo. This is like your K flag, and if purple striping becomes greater or occurs near the top of the plant, you should start to think about everything you are adding with a decent K value. The soil mixes in this book are well supplied with K so no worries there, you won't run out of K. Coconut coir fiber in the brick form, or coir that has not been rinsed, can both bring on a potassium problem slowly, and so can the overuse of powerful homemade TLO style earthworm castings. Keep your ratios as I suggest and you will be fantastic!

Organic Acids Overdose in Living Soil

I used a nice little dose of a liquid organic (OMRI rated) fertilizer on this plant when she was healthy, and even though I never used it again, within five days this is what she looked like. Just don't do this peeps, please don't read and believe all the bullshit about liquid nutrients regarding how they will "help" to do things you want to have happen—

Organic acid overdose in TLO soil

huge yields, etc. They are counterproductive in a living supernatural soil mix and the drastic pH drop will kill huge amounts of your microbeasties (and mini beasties) and compensating for this by using a pH Up product as a countermeasure (this is synthetic mindset thinking) will just make things worse with a vast introduction of *powerful* K salts.

Hermaphrodites

Thank you to Ocanabis for the excellent hermaphrodite photos here. Hermaphrodites (hermies) are a problem from time to time, caused by genetic sexual mutation from incompetent breeding practices, or by light leaks (light poisoning) during the plants' lights off time. Hermies can also be "normal" for some genetics that are landrace types and it is not uncommon for landrace cannabis varieties to express a true hermie female here and there along with perfectly sexually normal females; this is where things like breeding skills will favor your outcome.

Plants that have endured high stress levels during flowering can show sexual mutations (hermies) as well. Hermies are a survival adaptation that cannabis has developed to ensure propagation should highly unfavorable or "confusing" situations arise. Don't create these situations, and if you see the banana hermies later in flowering, check

Banana type hermie expression

thoroughly for "new" light leaks or light poisoning from an LED light on a power-strip in the flowering room/tent Feminized cannabis genetics and selfed cannabis genetics can develop this banana expression to varying degrees and will be faster or slower to show the bananas relative to the stress she is under.

How fast the plants are to react to stress with the expression of the bananas will have to do with a couple things I know of: First, how many times the plant has been propagated using hermaphrodite pollen in the recent past (6 or 7 generations back). Second, what type of stress causes the plant to react? For example light poisoning is a powerful stress source, confusing the plant as to which "season" she is in and almost any plant will react to light poisoning with a banana hermie expression. The plants will actually show the bananas about 7-14 days AFTER the light poisoning event began or happened once. Other things can cause bananas, like drought stress even, especially in those plants that are quicker to use the hermies as a response due to what I said just above.

The good news is, regarding the banana hermies, that if you find and stop whatever it is stressing the plant into hermies, most genetics of quality breeding will stop expressing these bananas within 10 days of fixing the problem. The bad news is, your resin production will always take a small hit whenever banana hermies show up, period. If you spot a few bananas before they pop any pollen, and you pluck them out with tweezers carefully, and these bananas were caused by your light leak error or other hard stress you caused and have identified and fixed, just keep looking and plucking for about a week or ten days past the fix and she will likely stop expressing bananas—again, dependant upon sexual qualities of the genetics. If she just goes mad throwing out many bananas, I would kill her immediately.

> **REV'S TIP** Bananas are a sexual mutation "programmed into the plant" where the plant is turning female calyxes into male flowers and they can be spotted fairly easily by their signature "waxy" look, and once you have spotted them once, they will always be much easier for you to see at a glance.

In the photo of the "true" hermie expression you can see much more normal looking male flowers, with female flowers on the same plant (at the same node and part of the same flower) and you can also see this plant is at a fairly early stage of flowering maturity. These kinds of hermie expressions are almost certainly genetic in nature, and this genotype is (favors) prone to using hermaphrodites to procreate.

PHOTO: OCANABIS

True hermie expression

These type of hermies show up normally soon into the flowering period and are not caused by external stresses. Hermies are very ancient, and they don't always obey rules; they are capable of amazing things, so far though none of those things are really good for a cannabis grower. True hermaphrodite plants are simply more (hermie) evolved versions of the sensitive banana hermie expressing plants. Hermaphrodites have simply worked too many times compared to normal sexual propagation, successfully, so now the plant completely favors using that (proven) method to reproduce—go with what works best, another truth of nature regarding evolution.

You can have a very normal (sexually normal) female plant, and if you know how long she flowers for, and she is exceeding that known flowering time by a week or more, whether you see banana hermies or not, you will want to investigate thoroughly for light leaks. Some genotypes (not many) I have seen under light leaks during flowering will never show any hermie expressions (that I ever saw and no seeds); but they will seem to "endlessly flower" still pushing out white pistils and kind of strange looking (sometimes) flowers, so if you see anything like this in your gardens look around closest to the plant(s) affected for the light leak.

TLO RESOURCES OVERVIEW

One of the really big bonuses about growing TLO style is that most of the products you will need are the exact same things any skilled all natural gardeners would need. So, if you are in a cannabis unfriendly state you still stay all low profile, as opposed to going to the hydro store and buying hydroponics nutrients (which is very telling). I get a bunch of my stuff locally at a local feed and gardening store, a lot of my bulk things like kelp, blood, bone, and alfalfa meal, and they also carry vermiculite and perlite. Walmart, oddly enough, has the best self watering growing pots I think so that's where I go for them. Wander around some of the gardening sections of your local stores and you might be surprised what you can find.

Pretty much everything else you want for TLO growing can be found online; and I actually use Amazon for a lot of fringe additions like my soft rock phosphate and granular Azomite. If you are going to be forced to pay some shipping then I advise you to get whatever it is in a decent size to save yourself some money from having smaller amounts shipped more often. Over at www.tlosoils.com my buddy D can help you out with some TLO soil mixes pre-made & supplies as well. Learn to compost yourselves – seriously, do it if possible, because skilled composting (worms or not) is truly magical goodness.

As far as lights and tents and whatnot, I like light shopping online pretty exclusively. Get a PO Box and have everything sent there if you want low profile status. My water filtration is online sourced as well. Clone King Cloners are available easily online for about $65.00 USD and work really well for me. Digital timers can be found in any larger store, or hardware stores, or online—don't attempt to set these while baked—Happy Trails.

CHAPTER 13

Sourcing Additions for TLO Gardens and TLO Hash Production

This TLO gardener has a healthy batch of additions for their garden

I get several of my really "exotic" things online, and other things locally in my hometown or very nearby. You can find a lot of things at local feed stores that supply local farmers, and crushed oyster shell is a favorite thing farmers use to supply their live chickens with calcium, so you just need to rinse these off to remove any residual sea salts, and they are normally really inexpensive. Make sure they have had nothing added to them, always! I get a 50 lb. bag for something like $7 at my local feed supply shop, and I use them all the time. I also get my granular rock phosphate from this same place, along with many of my growing containers, and most of my guanos and other Down to Earth products.

Local hydro-type stores are another place you can usually source some things you need for indoor TLO growing, like myco fungi stuff in bottles, expanded Cocogro coconut fiber, and often things like Fox Farm's Big Bloom liquid, bulbs, meters, and dry nutrients that are actually organic too. Have a look around in yours and get what you want to, but bear in mind that this source is normally the most expensive; read any labels carefully if considering new products. One of my local hydro-shops is really cool, and they order my Organicare Coir (expanded and rinsed) product for me if they are out.

Some things that I have to buy online are the more obscure additions like my powdered soft rock phosphate (micronized), powdered Dolomite lime, powdered gypsum. Check out the TLO supplies at www.TLOSoils.com. He carries *most* of the TLO specific elements that are hard to find. Don't substitute stuff all willy-nilly without knowing exactly what you are doing or you could cause yourself huge problems. You wouldn't want to do something like replacing the oyster shell product with additional Dolomite lime, for example. This move would likely end up killing your plants, due to too much magnesium in your soil mix, which is always a bad thing. There are many mistakes to be made by subbing out things with other things, and not knowing what you are doing. Always be very sure about this if you end up doing it. Here are some great sources for the things you'll need, including places online that have always been super helpful to me.

I get things like my pelletized/granular dolomite lime at a local Fred Meyer store, and many things from a local animal feed and gardening shop, some online etc. so just look for the best deal to you, and get some of the things you will be using more of in bulk, if you are getting them online to save in shipping costs over time. Just make sure to have some larger airtight containers to store them in bulk. Things like powdered gypsum and Dolomite lime will turn into big pieces of "concrete" rocks exposed to any kind of humidity over a little time in the open. So save some shipping and get things like the dolomite, or gypsum powdered, or whatever you need to get, online and think savings over time.

Some Down to Earth microlife inoculates

Microbial Life in Bottles

You can get Great White online at Amazon.com or in most grow shops. If you are using fresh living earthworm castings and/or are recycling your soil mix, then you have a whole bunch of beneficial bacteria, fungi, nematodes, and protozoa already present (and evolved if using recycled soil mix TLO style) in your living soil mix. However, you always need to add the myco fungus, and I use Great White powdered dry exclusively these days. The Great White is a high-quality microbial amendment, and I have never even heard of any not working great. It is a tad expensive, but worth it I think. The Great White has it all: bacteria, fungi, and myco fungi. Using the granular or other versions pay attention to how old the product is since packaging—*wink*.

Ground Oyster Shell

Down to Earth brand makes a great version of this product that is the consistency of course sand and it works great. Online this is easy to get and any nursery or grow-shop that stocks Down to Earth products can easily get it for you if they don't carry it normally. This stuff is just fantastic, and puts a real decent amount of great *slow-release* calcium into the living TLO soil mix. It also works great as a pH buffer (not a true buffer like Dolomite but helps keep pH higher rather than lower) and it helps to keep the other soil mix fungi from becoming too dominant as it really helps out the good bacteria, due to its influences on the pH and its porous nature. The ground oyster shell is a finer grade than the crushed version and I use both versions all the time, especially in my earthworm farm and when recycling soil.

Crushed Oyster Shell

I get my crushed oyster shell locally from my animal feed store, and being on the coast makes this product very accessible to me, so get this crushed shell if at all possible. If you get it straight from your local oyster farm, just rinse the shells off to remove excess sea salts. This product has become much more available since the release of my original TLO book.

Humic Shale Ore
(Humate Soil Conditioner)

I source mine locally, and many nurseries actually carry a lot of Down to Earth products. If not, you can usually convince them to start stocking something you will buy regularly, or at the very least they will special order it. Paying for the shipping gets a little pricey. I have made up batches of the TLO soil mix *not* using this product, and both times I did it I noticed a slight drop in vigor and plant size/growth rates (so, yields as well.) I'm sold on it, but if you just can't find it anyplace, you can leave it out.

Dolomite lime with pH information

Note the white granular nature of the dolomite lime

Dolomite lime

Prilled Dolomite Lime and Powdered Gypsum

I get both of these locally, and any good nursery should carry both; but they are both available online if you have to go there. Granular gypsum will work too; if only granular gypsum is available use double, or triple—depending upon granular size—the recommended amounts stated in the TLO soil mixes. Prilled Dolomite lime is fantastic, and the prilled form is just a pelletized form, usually reddish brown, and it will be granular looking and say "fast-acting" on the bag. The granular type of Dolomite lime that looks like rock salt will also work fine here too; it will just not be quite as effective (longer term) as prilled. Avoid the solid little rocks of Dolomite lime, and this will not say "fast-acting" anywhere on the bag.

Soft Rock Phosphate Powdered and Granular Rock Phosphate

Soft Rock Phosphate (SRP) powdered, and Rock Phosphate (RP) both are fairly tricky to source. SRP is a bit tougher, but better nurseries should

Rock phosphate bag	Rock phosphate application guide	Rock phosphate and dolomite lime

carry it, and they can certainly get it. Again you can source these online if needed, and I highly recommend you are using at least one of these grades in your TLO soil mixes. If you can only get the SRP then do that, but the RP is really a great addition and when recycling your soil mix you will really get the most out of the RP; so try to source that one as well. RP & SRP are the same mineral just different grades basically.

Perlite

Hydro shops and grow shops both usually stock this one. Higher end nurseries and even the Home Depot I used to live near carried this

product. You will usually find it in 4-cubic-foot bags for around $25.00 (USD), and you can find it in smaller bags too in places like Fred Meyer or in Kmart type stores in the gardening section. Also, with a little bugging you can easily get a local nursery to carry some or order it in for you. You need this addition, so go to whatever lengths you need to, because nothing I know of can replace it in container growing with a living soil mix. The microlife eats everything else too fast, like

Horticultural perlite bag

coir fiber and even shredded bark. Vermiculite will not sub out for the perlite quite as well, so don't go replacing the perlite with vermiculite only. You could use a 50/50 vermiculite/perlite blend for better water retention. Try and get the small nugget size grade of perlite and this is basic math; smaller particles equal greater surface area, and greater surface area equals better aeration. If you can only source the vermiculite for some reason then it is far better than nothing.

Greensand

This one can be hard to find in certain places, but fear not, because you can get it online in a 7 lb. box (Down to Earth brand) for about $12.00 (USD). But for real, any good nursery should carry this one and I have seen it in plenty of grow shops as well. Cannabis loves her greensand, so do what you need to do to get some of this. In a living soil mix it has many benefits beyond potassium and iron. I also add greensand to my earthworm food. If I couldn't get this locally, or have it ordered for me locally, I would get a large bag of it online so I would have it for a nice long time; but hey, that's me. Get it however you can, but *find* a way.

Compost and Earthworm Castings Teeming with Microbeasties

Fresh compost will always be the best, but you have to be sure the person making that compost knows a bit about what they are doing. Bagged compost is all fine and good, just avoid sterilized versions if possible, and

you should be able to find this one easily at any nursery. If you want to start making your own compost just get one of the compost tumblers as seen in this book and it will make your job much easier and your compost much faster to make. Bagged compost that is just a bunch of wood chips is sub standard and will not result in supernatural harvests.

Earthworm castings are a little harder to find, and lately I have seen these "designer castings" that are outrageously priced and are actually 50% coconut fiber. Full of life for sure but *dayum* they're expensive!

My personal worm farm
in my shed

Fine results can be had using this fast mix

Check your local nurseries and have them order worm castings for you if you can't find them because shipping will be a lot of money for a 20 lb. bag. Avoid sterilized versions of these, and live worms in the castings indicate all is well! I would just go ahead and pull the trigger on a small home earthworm farm, they really are "the shit" and since I got mine I have even started eating healthier to make sure my worms get good scraps; a double-whammy of benefits. Also, Gardner & Bloome (G&B) makes a rocking good bagged earthworm castings product full of life!

Home Earthworm Farms and Red Wiggler Worms

I can't recommend one of these more highly, and you can get them in a few places online like: http://www.homecompostingsolutions.com and that's actually where I got mine, and another good version is the

360° Vermicompost System. The 360 version takes up a bit more space, but is great for outdoors in a garage or shed—or even in a tent outside! You can also get your Red Wiggler worms here, and you really want these specific worms for TLO growing. Earthworms from your outdoor veggie garden will not like these farms. Warning: there may be a few gnats or fruit flies buzzing around near one of these worm farms, so if you are a bug-phobic person you should consider this. There are no bad smells as long as you add *perlite* and oyster shell to the worm food—a lot of perlite added to the worm food is a *huge* key to making these little earthworm farms not smell bad and perform supernaturally—keeping them too wet will also get them stinky and buggy!

Water Filters

Here is the direct link to my favorite place for all your water filtering needs, and I have been using this source for over a decade now and couldn't be happier with the products and the customer service:

LINK: www.purewaterproducts. com/countertop-ro

You will want the (Style A) countertop model from Pure Water Products (PWP) and make sure to ask for your *free* garden hose attachment. It comes with an attachment that fits most sink faucets included, but the additional garden hose attachment is priceless. You can just whip this filtering unit out whenever you need to make some pure filtered water and mine makes about 1.5 gallons per hour at my city's water pressure. It runs about $200.00 to your door and all ready to rock and roll.

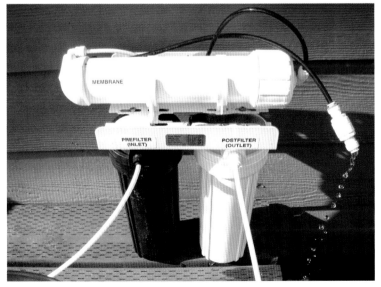

Countertop reverse osmosis water filtering unit (Style A)

Even apartment simple style will blow your mind if done correctly

Compost Tumbler

Here's the URL to my tumbler source and the size of my tumblers: www.amazon.com/Good-Ideas-EZCJR-BLK-7-Cubic-Foot-Compost/ dp/B002D925D6/

Otherwise just go to Amazon online and search for "compost tumbler".

Mine is the 7 cubic foot model, and I run it at half full. It is called the Good Ideas EZCJR-BLK 7-Cubic-Foot Compost Wizard Jr.

Simple Style TLO
a.k.a. Apartment Style TLO

This is a simple TLO soil mix to get your feet wet. You can use any good (high-quality organic) bagged soil mix like Fox Farms, or Gardner & Bloome, and just cut it with about 25% small-nugget perlite. You can super simplify spikes as well, and for your high nitrogen spikes use 1 part blood meal to 2 parts of kelp meal. For your flowering spikes use 1 part of bone meal to 1 part kelp meal; or, mix 1 part of high P bird/bat guano, to 2 parts of kelp meal. Get a good all-purpose type fertilizer like "Pure" granular by Organicare for layering, and you are set to rock and roll. How easy was that? Now this is just to check it out, but I assure you if you pull off a good and actual TLO harvest done right, you'll likely be into it deep just like me and many others. This won't bring out the extra large yields using this mix but it will work just fine and your yields will be good as well but you will have to use larger container sizes than if using my custom TLO mixes.

If you are going to do it then do it right and make sure you aren't inadvertently adding any synthetic salts from synthetic-style nutrients. This will kill the microbial life, and will befoul the final product, so do it right and see the real difference. I highly recommend a myco

SIMPLE STYLE ALL NATURAL TLO MIX

- 3 parts of quality organic soil mix, like Ocean Forest, or G&B (approx 3 cubic feet US DRY)
- 1 part of high-quality worm castings (approx 1 cubic foot US DRY)
- 2 part (approx 1 cubic foot US DRY) of perlite (perlite/vermiculite 50/50 highly recommended)
- 1 part coconut coir fiber—expanded, and rinsed if necessary (approx 1 cubic foot US DRY). Use an additional part of soil mix if no coir is available.

fungi product like Great White used with this dynamic as shown in this book.

Just blend this together well and make sure it is moist and not soaking wet; and it's ready to use—no cooking necessary. You can add 1 cup of greensand if able, no cooking required; the greensand ratio is assuming you are making the same (ballpark) total amount as in the recipe above. 6 cubic feet of soil is about 4 normal bags of soil. So just do the math if you need more or less. Use this soil mix along with spikes, and layering, and with slightly larger flowering container sizes. You can also use teas and with all those combined forces at hand, I think you will get a fine example of why TLO herb is all the rave. Your results will be even better, using my soil mixes and recycling everything, much better; imagine that!

Sweet and elegant using TLO style

In really small living spaces like apartments, you can improvise in a lot of ways. Totes, plastic kiddy pools, cheap shower curtains and tarps can all be used in small spaces to mix, recycle, cook, and store things without making any real mess. Right now I am growing using tents in a very small extra bedroom, a few external special function tents, and an outdoor shed where I do my recycling and all that, but if I didn't have the shed I could still pull it off. I could even pull it off with using just a closet and a cloner someplace else if I had to. It is nice to have the room for sure, but you can make TLO work really smoothly even in smaller personal growing spaces, and a spare bedroom and part of a garage are about perfect for a personal garden. TLO is very flexible, and you could set up huge greenhouses or warehouses on dripper systems or you could just fire up a couple of grow tents in your garage. I like tents a lot because you can have rooms full of tents as long as the rooms are dim and no light leaks happen—assuming you are using known quality tents like Jardin (lighter equipment tent style) or Hydro Hut (heavier equipment tent style).

In the recipe above, we are using a very simple synergy, combining the soil influencing (and fortifying) properties of the worm castings, the coir, and the greensand as well. You can learn about all those components in this book to see why this works. Combining things for a living soil mix is like having a bunch of random musical notes, and composing a song—a supernatural song. Once you start to get it, many things will just become obvious; if you screw it up, figure out what you did, and do it again "evolving" past that previous mistake. Anyone can give up easy, and this really isn't hard with this book; good luck on your mission.

True Living Organics Online Supplies and Ready Made Blends

Now, if you are thinking, "Damn Rev, I really want to grow this level of cannabis, I just don't have the time or space to do all these things,"—fear not good peeps, Daniel Callaghan over at TLO Soils can set you up with all the recipes in my book, and he does it right! He also is a one-stop shop for TLO supplies for doing it yourself.

URL: www.TLOSoils.com

PARTAKING OF YOUR TLO AMBROSIA

These days I prefer a couple of tools that each allow me to enjoy what I believe to be thee apex connoisseur's delight when partaking of TLO grown herbs and TLO dry sifted hashish. I am not really into wax/shatter etc. due to my belief that they are crap, and full of crap; however, if your Shatter is the result of dry sifted then heated product, with no bullshit added, then it's all good. If the only question were, if I will get high or not only, then some Raid Ant & Roach Killer on my buds would surely pack an extra punch. Take a step back maybe, check out what nature can do with a little help; actually and truly helping the natural processes. TLO herbs and hash is all about what's NOT in it, ya follow?

This is from Daniel: "We provide all of The Rev's recipes pre-cooked and ready to grow. We carry all the components needed to start your TLO grow successfully. We provide grow support for any TLO grower looking for advice or solutions to problems they are having along with a YouTube channel with tips, tricks and techniques."

Portable/Rechargeable vape pens are the best way I have ever experienced when smoking hash; and I use an Atmos Raw pen, for hash smoking exclusively. I never use it as a vaporizer and I just place little hashish balls right onto the heating element (omit the glass spacer for vaping). From a small BB sized piece of dry sifted TLO hash I get easily 4 large hits, and flame never touches my hash; which is nice. Under 100 bucks USD for these as a rule of thumb.

Atmos raw vape pen for elegant hashish smoking

For the best vaping experience I have ever had using TLO cannabis flowers, it's hands down, using my PAX Portable/Rechargeable Vaporizer, for vaping all my TLO flowers. These units will run you a little coin ($225.00 USD) but I have to say here, in my opinion, well worth the price. I have had mine for more than 2 years now and it gets used almost everyday, and I still couldn't be happier with it. There's a newer version that retails for about $280.00 USD—yikes—but still, it's a very high-quality tool.

Just at least use new (or clean) glass for your first TLO puffing experience. Avoid using an old dirty glass pipe that has had a lot of synthetically grown herbs smoked from it. Clean any dirty glass wicked well, so you can get a real grip on the HUGE difference in quality. Or go with my old time favorite—*doobie time!*

Vaping your cannabis flowers means simply controlling the heat very accurately allowing *only* the resin to become vaporized and be inhaled and not burning the actual flowers. So you are only partaking of the pure resin, period. When you are smoking hash, you are only smoking resin, period. So using the pen and the PAX consuming hash

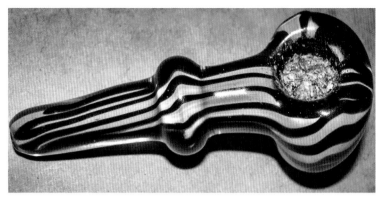

Good clean glass

and cannabis flowers respectively, you are getting the purest form of concentrated cannabis; just the resin. Actually, smoking cannabis flowers after using a quality vaporizer like the PAX seems almost crude by comparison to me now; so "be thee warned."

Tolerance

I want to say here, concerning the PAX Vaporizer, that if you are a very heavy consumer of cannabis, the PAX will likely not be a good idea for you. If you consume between say about 1 gram to 3 grams a day or less, it will be outstanding. Otherwise you may find it is a bit of a hassle to keep it always charged and clean. I love my PAX and these days I consume about a doobie's worth, or maybe two, or (sometimes) three a day; but, whenever I start needing more, just to feel the same great effects, I just stop consuming cannabis for a few days and knock my tolerance back down. I used to be able (30 years ago) to smoke a whole vial of prime Honey Oil a day easily, and if I didn't have any oil I would consume ¼ oz a day easily; so you can jack your tolerance way the

PAX vaporizer

hell up, and it's just a waste of good resin if you ask me.

Another way to combat your tolerance and to be able to keep your consumption from needing to climb constantly in order to have the same effects on you is to change things up. By this I mean have a couple or several varieties of cannabis on hand, allowing you to switch them up and when one variety starts to wane in effects due to your tolerance, simply start consuming a different variety for a day or two. This works the very best with at least one being a mostly sativa, and the other being a mostly indica.

I mention tolerance for several reasons, some obvious and others maybe not so obvious. Once you start to really "get" the TLO philosophy, of how things work in nature, you will automatically understand a deeper truth about tolerance. It's just how nature works, all living things naturally develop tolerances, it's evolution baby! So just let that roll around in your dome for a while as you learn why TLO works so well; it's because nature works well—*who knew*?

TLO STYLE DRY EXTRACTION (FROZEN CO2) HASHISH

Included in this book I wanted to share a somewhat different way to extract high quality hash very inexpensively, efficiently, and fast—like 30 min total to make 10-15 grams—with things you can just get at your local stores. This is a dry extraction method using nothing but frozen CO_2 to separate the little trichomes from the buds they are attached to. This method is the clean way to make your concentrates, and while I usually just use the lower buds or seeded buds from a plant to make my hashish this way, you can use sugar-leaf trimmings, or even buds that are mite or mold blasted pretty badly if you have those issues. I did an extraction article similar to this way back in SKUNK Magazine using fake ice cubes. However, this is the best way in my experience, and it has evolved. Blaze a fatty and I'll give you all the latest run-down.

Very stinky and
stunning to smoke

Standard pull from just
about one oz of buds

What You Need Before You Start
Nylon Fabric

If you have to, you can use pantyhose for this to strain out just the tri-chomes (trichs), however I would get a stronger nylon fabric because the pantyhose break down fairly fast and will sometimes tear, allowing pieces of the vegetable matter to get into your dry sift. This won't ruin it, but it is better to have pure trichs for top shelf hashish. You can gauge the fabric size by eye—I do. Just get a couple different ones the first time, then simply see which works best; you won't lose any trichs. If you use pantyhose I recommend you bust up your dry ice into smaller chunks, as larger chunks of dry ice can tear the thin pantyhose fairly easily. Also, remove as many stems as possible.

You want this fabric to be of the (micron) size that allows the maximum trichomes through while allowing no leaf or vegetable matter to get into your pure extract. Like I said, just have a couple versions of what looks right to you. One of them should be it and I have gotten very good at eyeing this type of fabric; you too will get this skill. It is a skill I recommend highly—*wink*.

Grown herbs reach peak potency when done well

Standard nylon fabric I use

A Small Heating Pad

This is a standard like 1 foot x 2 foot heating pad for placing underneath where the extraction happens in order to bring the temperature up of the freshly removed trichomes for better workability into hash balls. It is imperative you compress the extracted trichomes (trichs) into balls, or whatever as quickly as possible, because loose trichomes degrade quickly in light, exposed to open air. Especially where potency is concerned. You want this pad to just gently warm the tray you are using to extract upon, and this makes the hashish balls you hand make (or using a hash press is another option) very pliable to work with while compressing.

Heating pad underneath collection tray

The heating pad is one of the new additions I have come to rely on now, because due to contact with the CO_2 the trichs will be harder to meld together. But once in contact with the tray—via wax paper—it only takes a short time for it to become very workable. This step also helps remove any moisture that might be present and the results are rock hard deadly hash.

Dry Ice

This may be hard for you to get, however a little looking around and I bet almost anyone could find some nearby to them. I get mine from a local Fred Meyer grocery store, but I have other options if I need them, and I am way out in bum-fuck nowhere land myself. I get about 1 or 2 pounds of dry ice for a session and it's cheap, about $1.25 per pound (USD). I just have a small little personal size cooler I put inside when I get it to bring it home in.

This KOS variety will clean your clock

About a pound of dry ice

Insulated Gloves, Small Hammer and Freezer Bags

Insulated gloves are a must have for handling the dry ice and the shaker container while extracting the trichs. Seriously respect the coldness of the dry ice, as it is way the hell colder than water ice (dry ice is minus 109°F) and can cause you damage—guess how I know? Make sure you have some thicker, insulated gloves for this whenever you are handling the dry ice or anything like the baggie, or shaker container—ESPECIALLY the shaker container! Don't neglect this please, my esteemed homeskillets.

Thick gloves—hammer—ziploc freezer bag

Metal shaker containers work best

The Shaker Container

You can get these at Walmart or basically any store with kitchenware type items. I like the metal ones, and the one I use is about ½ gallon size; these are sold for holding sugar and flour etc. This sucker gets UBER COLD while shaking out the trichomes, so obey the law of the gloves while shaking out the trichs. These are very inexpensive; a few bucks tops in my local stores.

Your Herb of Choice

Now you can use sugar leaf trimmings, or buds messed up by mites or mold, or seeded buds (de-seeded or not) or killer buds. The better the quality of the herb that goes in, the better quality of hash that you will end up with, period. It is important that the herb be dry, and if stored for more than a few weeks before you make hash, be certain the herbs are stored in a cool, dark place in an airtight container. If you are using buds, don't break them up until just before you make your hash. Treat and store the buds like you were planning to store them for smoking, over time.

However, if you really want to produce massive amounts of deadly knock-you-on-your-ass hashish, use Hashplant/Kush types, because, dayum! On the flipside of the coin, many killer sativas make some down right spooky hashish that is tremendously potent with very long "legs" (length of influence). If you had a severe mite or mold invasion, the mites don't make it through the nylon fabric; however, I imagine mold spores could make it through the fabric. So if serious mold was your problem, you may want to use other options. I myself have extracted hash from a friend's buds at his house and he had pretty bad powdery mildew. I smoked a lot of that hash and did not pick up any hint of a moldy aspect. I myself don't fear smoking it too much; my greater fear lies in smoking what peeps use to fight it, yikes.

Let's Make Some Hashish

#1: Get a tray of larger size that's appropriate for your run. I use a 2 foot x 3 foot tray for this. Set it on top of the heating pad and turn on the heating pad; if your tray is thicker or insulated you may need to use a medium high-ish setting but the medium setting usually works. Put some wax paper on top of the tray and let that all sit for at least 20 minutes. After 20 minutes the surface of the tray and wax paper should feel just slightly warm to your touch. You can use this 20 minutes to bust up your buds if you are using buds, removing any stems as these can cause damage to your fabric. Place the bud product into the shaker container. Bust up buds to a point where you could roll great doobies from it. I just do this by hand; the more broken up the better.

#2: For about an ounce or two of herbs, a single pound (*maybe* two) of dry ice is plenty. Place your dry ice in the ZipLoc freezer bag and use a hammer to bust it up into smaller pieces, and then just pour out the broken up dry ice into your shaker container on top of the processed herbs. Place a piece of your fabric on top and secure with a nice rubber band to help keep it tight during the shaking out. PUT ON YOUR GLOVES NOW!

#3: Grasp the shaker container—wearing gloves—as shown in the photo, so you are helping the rubber band keep the fabric taunt/tight, because if it gets too loose you could have vegetable matter spill out into your pure trichome extract and while this won't ruin it, it will make

Killer buds of course work the very best for hash making

While tray is warming up—process your buds

it less than top shelf hashish. Swirl it around and shake it up for about a minute, then tip it and continue to shake and swirl the container around as you watch those beautiful trichs spill out onto the wax paper. Using about an ounce of herbs takes about three minutes to fully shake out.

#4: Once all the beautiful trichomes are laying in your tray on the wax paper, simply place another tray on top and let that sit getting warmer for about 10 minutes. This will bring all the (very) frozen trichomes up to a pliable working/compacting friendly temperature.

#5: Now that it is warm, take out small amounts (I do about 1 - 4 grams at a time if hand compressing into balls) and compress them. If you

Dry ice after
being broken Up

Secure fabric with a good
strong rubber band

Dry ice on top of
busted up buds

are using a hash press you can use however much at a time you want. Just let the trichs stay on the warming tray underneath the cover between compressing grams. It takes about 2 minutes to compress one gram by hand. Boom! Pouring some of the loose trichs into the corner of a ZipLoc can greatly aid the compression into hash. When done you will have your hash all compressed (un-cured) and it can be smoked right then if you like.

Shaking out the trichomes

Take away however much you will compress at a time

Curing Your Freshly Compressed Hashish

The freshly compressed hash will be warmer than the air around it so it will be conducting moisture out of the hash—*physics*! At this point I usually place all the compressed hash into a bowl or something in a drawer for about 30 minutes, then it gets sealed up in a jar and placed into a dark place for about three or four days. When you break it out you will see how it has set very hard and gotten über-stinky too! It will also possess much more refined smoking properties, and increased potency, I think.

Note: *Some* genetics have resin properties that are not friendly to compression and the compressed hash will fall apart way too easily into powder. For these cannabis varieties you can just pour the sifted trichs right into some pure (cool, not cold, and NOT hot) water and stir it up for about a

Place a tray on top to cover loose extraction and keep it warm

minute. Then just strain it using a pressing screen or something that allows water but not trichs to pass through it. Then you compress it (removing most of the water) using a pressing screen fabric with paper towels on the outside. Then compress your hash and leave it out in a warm dry place for at least two days—boom! Problem solved.

> **REV'S TIP** Selecting the right nylon fabric is really much easier than you may think. Out of about six or seven I have guessed at judging by eye, I have been spot on at least five of those times. Once you find the one you like, just go back to the fabric store and get a bunch of it. After you extract your hash simply run the fabric underneath hot water to clean it completely and it's ready for the next extraction!

Smoking Your Cured Hashish

There are a million ways to enjoy your hash. If smoking it I really prefer a glass bong or pipe, unless I have my favorite electronic pen (Atmos Raw). I just break off small pieces and ball them up, place them in the pen (right on the heating element) and experience what I think is the best and most efficient way to smoke your hash. You can smoke it un-cured if you like; it just won't have all the punch (potency) and flavors that it will once all cured up. Enjoy amigos!

TLO ON A LARGE SCALE INDOORS OR OUTDOORS

If you are growing using containers then TLO applies to indoors or outdoor gardens. Going large scale outdoors with containers seems counterintuitive to me, but if I were going to do that I would definitely go drip system, and get backpack pressure sprayers for teas (low pressure). This is also how I would do something like a warehouse garden of container plants; however, indoors I would likely use teas via hand watering old school, since I don't use teas very often, it wouldn't be too much work. Don't run teas through drip lines!

In the earth, outdoors, just throw up raised beds, use clean clones or seedlings and fill the beds with Supernatural Soil Mix Recipe 2.2 or Recycling Soil Mix Recipe about 10-30 days before you plant in them optimally. Spike them if you want to (at the time of transplant) out where the drip-line is going to be towards the edges of the raised beds. After harvest, just shred and compost all above ground organic matter that is extraneous; stems, leaves, etc. Compost local shrubbery/bushes that appears healthy, and didn't die from disease or pathogens. You can also pile up alfalfa and tree leaves and compost that.

Don't dig up the roots at harvest. Just cut the stems at soil level and let the roots "cook" in the ground preparing valuable food (and aeration) for next year's plants—that's a fact, Jack! You can add barn-yard manure, greensand, chicken poop, rabbit poop, bat poop—the poops are endless! Your only job during the composting process is to go out and turn those piles over as often as possible. Every other day isn't too much but at least once a week. Let it sit for about 15 days before you turn it over the first time after piling it all up and make sure to get it wet. Then after the 15-day mark you have to start turning it about once every three or four days to really get it jamming with the magic of enhanced (aerobic) Mother Nature. Stuff like petite twigs and leaves are beautiful in these piles for aeration, so use them if at all possible. That's really it. Outdoors is easy!

If you didn't have raised beds you would just have to make compost piles on each potential plant spot, during the season *prior* to your first actual growing season. So this would be slower to begin. Once you have harvested one crop there, you don't have to make large compost piles any more. Smaller sizes will work fine because remember, those roots from the previous season plant have decayed and "cooked" into very available plant nutrients underground. This also saves your second season plants from having to bore through the earth so much with their roots, as they can follow last year's plant's root "tunnels" down into the earth. The path of least resistance, man! It works out to less energy your plants have to expend on tunneling through solid earth, so there is more energy left for flowering potential.

Your largest concerns outdoors are as they always have been: Security, plant eating beasties large and small and watering mechanics including sourcing good water. Figure out your whole watering logistics FIRST and implement them before the plants arrive on the scene. PVC and drip tubing are my mostest and bestest friends for this application. Gravity feeds work well with drip and no water is wasted—or at least, very little. It's pretty easy to keep it all fairly stealthy with a little digging of the trenches stuff, burying any tubing/plumbing, etc. Earth is quite capable of sustaining plants; look around. Security is the most important of all. Loose lips and all that too, deterring predators that would chow down on your plants, like caterpillars and deer to name two of many will also likely be a concern.

Water and watering is the real key to enhancing your outdoor grow, truly, once you have all the soil treated with the compost piles and last year's root networks underground. Just move out to the sides any left-over composted matter that is still not decomposed into smaller pieces. No worries, just mulch with it. The soil below the compost pile has now been "activated" with mucho diverse micro and mini life forms that will show you what this planet can do. If you grow enclosed

OFFICIAL TLO DRUID GERMINATION GUIDE

From seed to flower all TLO style all the time

Let's make a bet! Take 10 seeds or whatever, do half your way and half my way (exactly) and once these plants are about 30-40 days old, you will already be seeing the big differences. No need to believe me, see for yourselves the truth I be sharing with you all! Germinating is so very straightforward and simple when playing into the strengths of the living soil mix using the TLO methodology. I have done a bit about germinating earlier in this book, however since this seems to be problematic for many of you that have not done this too many times (or ever) I want to give you this additional guide to up your savvy here, TLO Druid style.

Healthy happy sprout in living TLO soil mox

or partially enclosed outdoor plants in very HOT regions, I would advise you to set up your water delivery via mini sprayers (avoiding spraying the main stem always) as this will really go a surprisingly long way to cooling off the whole plant. The plant will circulate the coolness and you will see mucho happier plants!

First a Few Words Regarding Germination Using Water and Paper Towels Etc.

Now I know lots of you growers out there, well seasoned, still use these methods revolving around soaking seeds in a glass of water and putting them into paper towels etc. I used to do the paper towels myself, like 10 years ago. It's not that I think these methods are "wrong" —not at all. What I do think is that playing into Mother Nature's strengths is far superior, based on the results I have seen side by side over the last decade of TLO growing.

The (Supernaturally) Living Soil Mix

I strongly believe now that the plant and the soil mix start their symbiotic bonding the moment the seed cracks open, likely even before that. Little sprouts have a very busy genetic-driven engine running right out of the gate, using inherent genetic driven adjustments to their makeup in order to most favorably adapt to their perceived environment. This

A healthy sprout about 8 days old

Germinating TV dinner
style container

includes their awareness of the variety of microlife they will be dealing with in order to get their maximum nutrient/element issue *from* that soil mix. You will see this for yourself expressed by your plants being larger, healthier and heartier than those plants germinated in paper towels; I certainly did, and still do.

One of the most important aspects I have come to really rely on is always preparing any soil mix for seedlings at least 24 hours in advance of using that soil mix. By "preparing" all I mean is blending a ready-to-rock soil mix with some additional earthworm castings at a ratio of about 80% soil mix and 20% earthworm castings. This actually hyper-inoculates the soil mix with microlife, ensuring that the plant has a nice (extra) wide diversity of life to interact with and a wealth of awesome organic matter.

You don't need to use a "mellow soil mix" for germinating seeds, and I highly recommend you sprout in the same basic soil mix the plants will be growing in. If you want to use just a bagged soil mix (they will need transplanted sooner using bagged) that's fine, but I highly recommend you blend it with earthworm castings as I mentioned above. Perlite is also an important amendment whenever growing in containers. Make sure your soil mix for sprouting is like your soil mix for growing with about 20-30% of it being perlite. This gives your soil mix the ability (via more aeration) to support more life, and as anyone who knows anything about the True Living Organics philosophy of growing knows, this will be able to support unusually high levels of microbial life in the soil mix. Supernatural levels, in fact, and that's the name of the TLO game mis amigos.

I use the flats or the "TV dinner" type trays (put drainage holes as in photo) to sprout in, and either works fine. I would recommend you transplant the little sprouts as soon as they are up out of the ground and opened up if using the TV dinner style trays. However, in the germination flats you can leave the sprouts for a week or 10 days before having to transplant them if you are using a TLO soil mix and not bagged. Make sure to clean whatever type of container you are using first; don't space this! As the plants get bigger and bigger, I also recommend you step up your containers sizes in small steps. This ensures that you will end up with a very dense root mass by the time you get up into flowering containers.

Healthy seedlings about 28 days old—same sprouting soil mix

Planting the Seeds

Let me start by saying I do touch my seeds with my fingers sometimes—I just try and do it as little as possible. Some believe oils from the skin have a detrimental effect upon the seeds. Myself, I can't say, but that's how I've been rolling for the last eight or 10 years and I always have 90%+ germination rates.

I use a spoon for all my transplanting of sprouts and it is my favorite tool for this purpose. You can just "cookie cut" them out of the TV dinner trays and scoop them up and out of the flats. Easy peasy! Be gentle to all the fragile life you encounter along the way, and just slide the spoon out from under the roots when placing!

You can see in the photo how deep of a divot I make to place the seed into. I just use the tweezers (this is a skill you will get good at) to place each seed, but then I press it down lightly with my fingertip (make sure the seed doesn't stick to your fingertip) before burying the seed with some additional soil mix, using the same as the soil they are planted in. Make sure to leave some space between seeds if using the TV dinner containers, so you can "cookie cut" them out before lifting the sprout out, using the spoon for both jobs. Tamp down the soil on top of the seed lightly and use a mister or turkey baster to moisten all, gently and thoroughly watering and not disturbing the soil. I would highly recommend you go out of your way to get a mister for this and many more reasons. Get one that is a true mister as in the photo. Mine is a Solo. Alternatively, I would recommend you use a turkey baster to gently water the planted seeds or the mister thereafter until they are transplanted. If you don't have a good pump mister or a turkey baster, I would get one of each ASAP. They're highly efficient tools of the trade for multiple applications.

Place your planted seeds under some intense lighting; this is very important for vigorous hearty sprouts. This is their formative time, dur-

Use tweezers to handle seeds

ing which they are judging their environment big time! I like to sprout under a photoperiod of 14/10 (14 hrs ON and 10 hrs OFF) and once they are two weeks above ground I up the photoperiod to 16/8, and then at 45-55 days above ground I go to an 18/6 photoperiod. This kind of represents to them what season it is and they perceive this as springtime, at least that's my philosophy regarding this.

Note: If growing all naturally or organically I would avoid using 24 hour ON photoperiods. This does not make for supernaturally happy plants in the long term, in my opinion.

If you cannot mimic these variable photoperiods, keep it simple and sprout them under your vegging photoperiod (example 16/8) but I *don't* recommend running a vegging photoperiod with greater than 16 hours on, as some genetics will tend to produce more males under longer photoperiods. My favorite way to do this is right in the flowering room/tent under the 12/12 photoperiod about three feet from my 400 watt Eye Blue Halide lights. You can leaves them under this 12/12 photoperiod for several weeks if need be. Getting good at sprouting some healthy and hearty plants is a huge boon to any grower.

Fingertip deep (about half way to the bottom of container) approx ¾ inch

Nutrients, Watering & Water

I don't know how to be anymore straightforward about this: DO NOT feed your sprouts with anything for at least 9 or 10 days. Nothing except good water—good water by all natural TLO growing standards. A mellow tea about a week after they sprout is fine just keeping it very mellow, but you don't need to do this at all. Over or under watering are the two main killers of little sprouts. Seriously, these mistakes with watering are critical.

REV'S TIP To inoculate your seedlings with mycorrhizal fungus, simply mix in some of the granular types with your seedling soil mix just before planting the seeds. Alternatively, you can use a water-soluble version like Great White on them a day or two after they first break ground, like I do.

This is Blue Rhino 1947 from KOS, TLO grown and beautiful

The mighty turkey baster—all hail

You must be vigilant, make sure there is aeration from above and below. You must maintain the "Goldilocks Zone" of moisture for the seeds, sprouts, and plants, all the way up the line. This is a skill, dial it in, make it a priority and you won't be sorry.

When I say "feed" what I really mean is feeding the living soil mix and I never recommend adding any kind of liquid nutrients to a TLO living all natural soil mix, but organic teas made on the mellow side are all good after a week or 10 days above ground, not before, it would likely not work out well.

I often use a turkey baster to water the soil before the plants break ground, and after, very delicately I dribble good water out all around them. Make sure your chosen containers are aerated from above and below, I used a wooden skewer broken in half to make some space between my germination tray and the inverted plastic plate you see in the photo. This also helps keep the plant up out of any standing water at their base, and make no mistake, standing water like this for longer than about 30 minutes is potentially detrimental and can cause anaerobic activity and kill roots—*not* good.

A quality pump mister

Use something to elevate germination tray

Additional Tips

You can sprout them in your flowering room under your flowering lights at a 12/12 photoperiod if you like. Try and keep them about 3 feet away from the bulbs, and remove them from that photoperiod after they are above ground for a week or three, when it's time to transplant them. You can go to a 16/8 photoperiod after the transplant; however, keep your lighting intense, and you will have some SERIOUS sprouts! Watch out for them drying out quickly under intense lighting.

Get a couple of turkey basters, as these have multiple usages around gardens: For measured gentle watering of clones or seedlings, sucking excess water from trays beneath small plants, aerating gallon containers of water by sucking out and blasting water back into the container. The list goes on and on.

I hope this helps those of you having issues with germination. It really comes down to two major things, *no feeding* for at least 7 or 10 days—and I only mean a mellow tea when I say feed—and moisture/water control. Master your control over any urges to "feed" your sprouts with any kind of liquid nutrient—*big mistake*—and just don't let them dry out too much or be too wet for too long and you'll rock it.

RECOMMENDED FURTHER READING FROM THE REV

Teaming With Microbes
This was written by Jeff Lowenfels and Wayne Lewis. One of the greatest books I have ever read, it really comprehensively explains what "all natural" really means; a must read in my opinion. It's all about teas and how the plant really runs the show, and it's full of useful and mind opening information. A must have for TLO enthusiasts and all natural-style growers everywhere.

Marijuana Botany
This was written by Robert C. Clarke. This is also a must have, and it covers everything from simple to complex, start to finish. Comprehensive and great for referencing subjects fast, if you do not have this book and you love to grow cannabis, I advise you to score this puppy now! You'll thank me.

The Cannabis Grow Bible
This was written by Greg Green from Green Candy Press, and is the one I always refer peeps to when they want a general all about and how-to guide when growing cannabis. I think this book is awesome.

The Soul of Soil
This book is a great eye opener and full of fascinating information about soil. It's not really about indoor gardening at all but it is outstanding and comprehensive, and it's sure to enhance your perspective in your own gardens indoors and out.

Earthworms Eat My Garbage
This was written by Mary Appelhof and is a must read in my opinion for TLO recycling related info.

You want a worm farm you say? Get this book my green friends, and it will really open your eyes to the world of worms, which is the entire world; at least how the world works. There is an amazing amount of info about building and maintaining your own indoor worm farm like mine.

Index